CAMBERWELL BOOTY –

a young totter's war efforts

David Lillywhite

Published by David Lillywhite
Publishing partner: Paragon Publishing, Rothersthorpe
First published 2022

ISBN 978-1-78222-915-5

Book design, layout and production management by Into Print
www.intoprint.net
+44 (0)1604 832149

Contents

The Butterfly 'Camberwell Beauty' was identified and named by one Moses Harris in 1776. It was also known as the 'Grand surprise' and 'Mourning Cloak' and was found in Coldharbour Lane. Camberwell.

Samuel Jones, Makers of Adhesive Paper, adopted the 'Camberwell Beauty' as a Trademark for their factory in 1919 and it was incorporated in the high façade on the outside of the building in the form of a large mosaic. Many people thought it to be too prominent during World War II and may have been used as a Landmark for the German Bombers. The factory was demolished in 1982 and the mosaic was moved to the Library in Wells Way, Camberwell.

Foreword

There is no chronology in this calendar of events - subjects flit between the nineteen forties and fifties. I must plead my addled brain; it will be up to the reader to decide on the timeframe.

I have been cursed or blessed with a moderately good photographic memory. Many dyslexics and partial dyslexics like myself seem to have this kind of remembrance. In addition, even to this day, I am also regarded as slightly eccentric, someone who looks at life with dark and sardonic humour.

I was diagnosed (along with many flaws and 'isms') by the marvellous Maudsley Hospital as war-damaged. This condition included an awful stutter which has never quite gone away. However, meeting other kids of the same ilk at the Maudsley Hospital along with a speech therapist, helped enormously, letting us all know that we were not alone, our afflictions shared.

In my earlier years I had few friends, biding my own company. Friends were an option but I preferred keeping to myself. I was forever out on the streets of South London. Being allowed out only in daylight hours, I went home to a clean house with pretty good parents. A sister was added to the household, then we were four - no more. Amen!

Out on the streets of Camberwell I could be anyone that I chose to be, with no-one to contradict or challenge me.

This is my story, my journal. Read on.

The Day I Saw Our King and Queen

I **sat on top** of a tram stop at Camberwell Green waiting for the King and Queen who were coming through Camberwell any time now. I was late, only finding out at the last minute from some kids who were in the middle of a "war game". When I found out, I quickly hid my handcart in one of my secret hiding places.

I had been out all morning finding things like rags, metal and wine bottles, for which I received 2d each at Roses bleach factory at Peckham. I had found two VPs, one Wincarnis and two Green Goddess wine bottles, quite a catch. I'd made my cart from an old packing case, a couple of bassinette pram wheels and I'd found wood from some bomb debris sites for the shafts. After hiding my barrow, I raced to Camberwell Green only to find crowds of people, four deep. As no one would let me through to the front, out of desperation I climbed up the tram-stop, which was closer to the crossroads than the bus stop. My dad said tram-stops and bus stops have to be sited some distance apart because if they were together the buses and trams would clog the whole road up, causing a traffic jam. You see, my dad knows everything! Whatever I ask him he always has an answer because he MA-TRIC-ULATED at school, and should have had an apprenticeship with C.B. Corman making diving equipment, but my Gran and Granddad made him take a job with his brothers gully cleaning, using machinery. It was hard work and him with a weak heart (having contracted rheumatic fever as a child). I suppose the extra money was more important.

Anyway, the crowds were festive; King George VI and Queen Elizabeth touring round south east London today, Camberwell being one of the worst boroughs to be bombed. It wasn't just the east end of London, but all over! Still, it was late summer, and we were at peace.

My dad was an air-raid warden during the war, pumping water and clearing drains after the bombing. He would come home after work, change into his Air-Raid Warden's Kit, working through late nights pulling people out of caved-in houses, patrolling the streets, looking for whatever came along. One night he was sent home early, having pulled bodies from his best friend's house. He came home really early, because 'Itma' was still on the radio. He sat in front of his food, not eating but crying like a baby. I had seen people crying in the streets; I suppose everyone felt the same, not just anyone, but everyone. We just sat at the table quietly.

Anyway, I was getting a sore bum sitting on the tram-stop, wishing the King and Queen would hurry up. Like all kids, I was quite skinny, there again everyone was skinny, even grown-ups. One kid I knew at school, Stanley Crane, was quite fat. He told me, when I asked politely, his doctor told his mum it was GLAN-DU-LAR. I liked Stanley Crane, pity we weren't friends because he said nothing about my stutter, and I never said anything about his size.

Friends for me were out of the question. They would interfere with my finding things (sometimes before they were lost), also they would expect some of my hard-earned money.

What was I saying? The police were stopping the traffic so the King and Queen must be near, but I was feeling cramped.

I thought about the King's stammer, having seen him on the Pathe Newsreels, looking at the blitz areas, talking to people, giving comfort. He didn't seem to stammer at all, so when I told my Dad, he said that our King was "slow of speech" like Moses in the Bible who, when he did miracles, took his brother with him, to explain to the Egyptians what Moses could do, and what was going on. Someone told me that many famous people had stammers, even an old Greek poet. who tried to cure his stammer by filling his mouth with pebbles, and shouting at the sea – all this information helped me, I suppose, and now I know why the King didn't go pop-eyed, or purse his lips like I did. I really enjoyed talking to my Dad, who never said "spit it out", making me feel worse.

The Scribe

My Dad was quite famous where we lived in Westmacott Street, as well as Caspian Street, even Lomond Grove. He would write people's letters to the Courts, Landlords and sons in prison. My Dad would discuss with them their letter's content, then later he would write it up in the King's English. He also worked out people's winning betting slips for a small fee. Illegal bookies could not always be trusted!

Sometimes he was paid in kind, eggs, potatoes, whatever anyone could afford to give. I would watch him writing, amazed at the speed of his writing. He called it Copperplate. Block capitals rolled off his old fountain pen as fast as a tommy gun, each perfectly formed, all under our gaslight. I would sit and watch.

Our local Magistrate was a lady called Sybil Campbell, who called all local folk the "criminal classes". My Dad advised people to plead Guilty with EX-TEN-UAT-ING CIRCUM-STAN-CES, thus getting a lighter sentence. Most times, this worked. He also told me to stay "within the law" as I was becoming a streetwise urchin.

Mums would warn their kids who did wrong *"Sybil Campbell will put you in prison"*; people feared and hated her.

I took heed of what was said and was always careful not to be stopped by the police. Camberwell police station was known by all to be a bit "iffy".

Our local MP was Freda Corbet, Labour, who would sort out people's problems where she could. Everyone liked her. My Dad sent lots of his letters to Freda Corbet!

A cheer went up – they were here! Sitting in the biggest black car I had ever seen with the roof folded back like a carriage. The King was wearing a khaki uniform. I wondered what regiment he was in! The Queen was all in blue, looking radiant, smiling and waving. She looked up and saw me, waving so much that I nearly fell off my tram-stop. The King followed her gaze and smiled. I couldn't believe my eyes – a royal wave!

Later in my life, I read once that "the memory is a bad photographer and a good novelist". Be that as it may, I can still recall, to this day, that what I had seen on that special day was true!

The King and Queen were now heading slowly towards Kennington with their escort. The crowd did not move. *"Didn't they look well"* – *"She looked lovely"*. Finally, the crowds broke up, I climbed down from my tram-stop, elated. Cor, what stories to tell my Mum and Dad; what a day.

On the way home I checked my barrow, it was still hidden – good. I would carry on "totting" tomorrow. Walking home, I thought about all the things I had remembered in my long life. I was about eight years old or so as I sat on that tram-stop. Probably only minutes had passed but with my stutter, it would take me ages to tell my Mum and Dad, my

Gran and Granddad what I had seen. Well, no one's perfect, are they?

My Mum was a saver, my Dad was not. Some time before I was born, my Mum started to put money aside for my pram, and other money for housekeeping, and money for the rent. She made little piles of her savings, put in special places on the mantle shelf, out of my Dad's way – she disapproved of his gambling.

My Dad had a good name as a bets settler. He could settle instant bets a lot faster than any machine, being clever. One bookie called Ike took a shine to my Dad – he had worked out some complicated bets, saving him a lot of money.

The World Heavyweight Contest between Joe Louis, a brown American and Max Schmelling, who was German and a member of the Master race. Everyone thought that Schmelling would win, but most people liked Joe Louis better. He was a quiet person who was known as the *"Brown Bomber"*.

Ike, the bookie was Jewish, and he knew that Joe Louis was going to knock Schmelling out in round one of the match, telling my Dad that it has become a racial matter, and "swore my Dad to secrecy". My Dad trusted Ike, who said "put all that you can raise on Louis in the first round to win, but do not put the bet on with me". My Dad took my Mum's savings, picked the lock on the gas meter, and emptied it, leaving an IOU. He then pawned his suit, borrowed from friends, putting all this money onto Joe Louis to win in the first round, which he did. He paid everything and everyone back, including the gas meter, bought a really posh pram, flowers, loads of food and drink and a present for my Mum.

It was the boxing match of the century – Max Schmelling knocked out in the first round! My Dad was nearly knocked out in the second round by my Mum. She went mad at him for gambling her savings on a silly boxing match. Some things you can't win, can you?

Recyclers

Oh yes, on the other side of our street there lived the Ludlows; the Dad, Joe, was a full-time totter. His trolley or cart was well kept; the woodwork was scalloped and painted like the Gypsies' caravans. Every afternoon he would come back fully laden. Ruth, his big fat wife, sorted out the cast iron from the steel, sorting out what was lead, copper and zinc.

Boy, did she know her metal! She would tell him what it was worth, on account that Joe couldn't read or write or add up. He would come back empty and park outside where he would wash his horse, drying him off with some clean dry sacks. He would then lead his horse through their house, going through their front room, back room, through the scullery to their tiny backyard, to where Joe had built a kind of stable. The horse would be fed his oats and his drink for the night. One happy horse. Saturday was the horse's day off. On Sunday, if a fine day, Joe would bring the horse out in his best bridle. He would brush and comb the horse, who knew they all were going out for an excursion.

Ruth would climb up onto the trolley sitting by Joe – who had cleaned the trolley up. As they pulled away she, being big and fat, he, skinny as a rake, they looked from behind like a matchstick and matchbox, and trotted down

Westmacott Street, probably meeting with other totters for a Sunday drink.

Some people in the street looked down on Joe Ludlow, saying he wasn't clean. How stupid. Any man who washed his horse every day must wash himself. I ask you! It's obvious. He did sometimes smell of horse, but you would expect that, wouldn't you? I mean, we all smell of something.

I'd better get on with this – the Ludlows had an older daughter called Lou who was nice and plump; people were starting to put weight on a bit. She was known as a spinster – on account that there wasn't enough husbands to go around. Less men came back from the war than had left. Lou was always having parties for her very young brothers – always baking cakes and jellies, and giving us hugs. I hope she met someone in the end.

Nearly forgot, *"Red Biddy"* was drunk again on VP wine and was strutting down the middle of the street, her cloche hat on crooked, with lots of kids following, trying to follow her steps. She always sang the same song "I Don't Care What Becomes of Me". Her neighbours said it was depression caused by not having enough money to pay her rent arrears. Her real name was Mrs Story. I never saw any Mr Story or any little Storys, not even when the bailiffs came to take her furniture away in Sears Street, round the corner to us. The neighbours would be tipped off when the bailiffs were due, each household taking one or two of her possessions until the house was empty. I was there watching when the bailiffs went into Red Biddie's house. "Ficking 'ell, all the furniture's gorn!" Later the furniture was put back.

Did I say our street was famous! My aunt Claire lived in Canada in a city called Toronto. She was a Librarian and took classes in English Literature for children who were slightly behind at school.

One day she was looking at a magazine called National Geo-something. There was a large picture of Westmacott Street looking all the way down nearly to the end. The caption read A Typical Street in South East London. Aunt Claire could not believe her eyes. There was my Gran talking to Nell Godwin, her neighbour, Joe Ludlow taking his horse indoors, and the Pussy Butcher in the middle of the road!

Now the Pussy Butcher or cats meat man, sold horsemeat all around Camberwell and Walworth. He would buy a large piece of horse from the knackers yard at the Elephant and Castle, cook it in his shed, cut it up and wrap each portion in fresh newspaper, load up his huge basket then do his rounds. The local cats loved him, but he hated them. As he walked down our street, the cats would catch wind of his basket and would follow him in procession like the Pied Piper of Hamlin. He would turn and snarl *"HUCK ORF!"* – to make things worse they took no notice and even more cats joined in. Poor man. He wore the same black long overcoat summer and winter, the same dirty cap. You could have boiled them both and quite easily make horse soup from the proceeds.

At Camberwell Green we used a horsemeat shop for humans called a 'Continental Butchers'; as other meat was scarce, they did a good trade. The only thing was my Gran always cut fatty bits off because it was yellow.

My Gran was either born in India or went there as an army cook where she cooked for the 'Ranks' – officers and gentry – and soon learned Indian cookery.

During the last war, she always had hessian bags full of spices. I never knew where they came from, there were no Indians to buy them from. She looked after me sometimes and her curried horse was delicious.

Once or twice we had whale meat when there was no horsemeat, but the whale meat steaks were almost black and very tough, no matter how many times Grandad beat them with his hammer, they were still pretty tough after hours of cooking. Still, we survived somehow.

After the war, rationing got worse, the USA were stopping sending us food now that the war was over 'cos some people were Profiteering'. Mr Truman, their president, said enough was enough. Down our street, everyone was complaining.

My Dad said "We fought in the war for freedom of speech, now all of us could have the freedom and the right to complain, even the Germans could moan, which they couldn't do under Hitler!" I think I understood.

I soon learned to shut my gob when people started moaning about food shortages. At the "flicks" Pathe newsreels showed everyone still sorting through the bomb debris, finding bodies, cleaning bricks, finding all kind of things, doing the same in England and in Germany. If I half closed my eyes and squinted at the screen, it looked just the same, exactly like the British doing similar things in our cities; there were German kids with carts just like mine. The War is over but I miss the American soldiers on leave walking around Camberwell Green, waiting to go and fight the Germans, their private soldiers on Embarkation leave, smart in their posh uniforms, all looking like officers. Our soldiers only had one uniform for everything, their cloth looked and felt like horse blankets. I bet they didn't half itch! The Americans were paid three times more than our soldiers, it was said.

The Yanks couldn't understand that our pound had 240 pennies, their dollar having 100 cents, so our shopkeepers could short change them easily. The Yanks soon caught on.

We would say to the Americans "Got any gum chum?"

There being no sweets in the shops to buy. Some would say "Frig off you Limey brat". Others would give us sweets called "Life Savers" in a tube, tasting of peppermint with a hole in the centre. They were great, taking away the taste of my mum's cooking. Yuk! They also called their sweets Candy! Strange. Some Americans seemed to be related to someone called Uncle Sam – I never did find out who he was.

They brought with them carpenters, engineers and lots of material – they could make anything for the war effort.

If there was any off-cuts they would make thousands of toys and gave them to us kids. I was given a wooden tommy gun. Now that I am eight years old, I'm too grown up for toys, but I treasured my tommy gun when I was younger. All the local kids got something.

My Mum worked at Trollop & Coles, who were once builders. Now their workshops were converted to making pontoon barges for the invasion. My mum couldn't cook well but she was a very good worker. She was soon given her own gang of women, spraying and finishing the pontoon barges. She was in her element wearing her fitted boiler suit, blue turban and work boots, doing a useful job. She also would slip out at lunch break to check our street after an air-raid. I was very proud of her, even though she couldn't cook.

What with my Dad working all day and half the night as an air-raid warden, I only saw my Mum and Dad together at weekends.

Alma Mater 1

A fter the war was over some things returned to normal. Our junior school was reopened again having been taken over as a hostel for families who had been bombed out. There were dormitories for single people and space for families. Ratty Jarvis, our local rat catcher, was kept very busy and cleared rats from our temporary school at Camberwell Green called "Green Coats". It had been closed for ages. My Dad said it was Medieval.

After the rats had been caught and the old school had been cleaned, our class had no paper or textbooks so Miss Burke, the head mistress, managed to find us some "Old Moore's Almanacs" in a local shop, all dated 1938, all the same issue, so we all had to try and identify some of the words on a certain page. It was pretty hopeless. None of us could read anyway. Miss Burke did her best, but it was hopeless.

When the war was over, and things were being cleared up, finding things became a way of life. That was when I came into my own as a totter.

I s'pose that I should come clean about what happened at the 'George Yard'. It was a massive bomb site, stretching from Camberwell Road to Lomond Grove. Lots of people used it as a short cut to our street. At the front of Camberwell

Road there was one shuttered large shop still standing, despite the bombing, behind in the George Yard in a large garage full up with old Grey painted taxis, used by the fire services. It seemed to me that whatever the Government wanted, all they had to do was paint it grey! There was a high window with the glass blown out leading to the back of the shop, so I pulled my trusty barrow over, piled some boards on top, reached in and opened the window sash and being skinny, slithered in. Sometimes it paid to be thin, cos I was inside! The whole place was full up with old and new junk left over from the war; it was like Aladdin's Cave. There were hundreds of army gas mask bags, all brand new; inside each one had a pocket with a celluloid flat-pack set of goggles. Ideal for the "Albany Aces" cycle speedway team, who often raced in the George Yard. I could flog them easily and the bags would easily sell to men going back to work for their tea and sandwiches. I sold out.

On my third trip back into the shop, I was caught! Waiting for me was the biggest Copper in the police force. He grabbed me by the scruff of the neck. "Gotcher!" "Name?" Like a fool I told him my real name, I was so frightened. I had rehearsed the name Harold Hawkins to use if anyone asked. Jim Hawkins was my hero in an old film called *Treasure Island*, he was good at finding things too. I could say aitches without stuttering. L and S sounds always made me start to stammer, giving the game away. There was nothing I could do.

He looked at me and said "You can come along with me to the station and be charged, or you can deal with me here". My Dad had taken me to the Camberwell police station once to have me locked up for the night in a cell. My Dad explained what I had been doing, and wanted to teach me a lesson.

"We can't do that," the desk sergeant said, "we have to catch him first", but instead I was shown the inside of a holding cell. That was enough. I resolved to be more careful. I did not want to go before Sybil Campbell pleading guilty. That was when I had the idea of Harold Hawkins. Anyway, I said to the copper "I'll have it here" so the big copper smacked me on my ear wearing his big woolly glove, and let me go with a warning. It took two days before my ear stopped ringing.

I never went back.

My Debut Into Pawn, Or Visiting Uncle's

Sometimes I was in demand. Monday things would be pawned at Harvey & Thompsons on the corner of Bluff Place and Camberwell Road. During the last war, Lord Haw-Haw used to broadcast from Germany. He supported Hitler. People everywhere hated him. Once he broadcast that Germany would bomb Bluff Place and rid Londoners of the slums and criminals who lived there.

From the pawnshop you could see that there was not one house still standing. Well done, Lord Haw-Haw, but you still lost the War, you traitor.

Mondays and Fridays were pawnshop days. I would collect the parcels back, most people using the same brown paper and string over and over again.

I would load up my clean barrow to the brim, covering the top over with an old piece of cloth. Most people were shy about 'Uncle's' so that's where I came in. Harvey and Thompson had this big long counter. I'd give the man each person's money and the tickets, he would then go into the back where things were stored. He shouted a name, and threw the parcel at speed calling out a name I could not recognise; most of my customers gave false names and I couldn't keep track of who was who and whose were whose. To make things worse I was always taken to the ticket writing machine, (which had three pens, and three inkwells attached to a gimbal). When the pawnbroker wrote tickets I was so obsessed by seeing the other two pens working by themselves, I would often be knocked over by a heavy sliding parcel. "Wake up, it's one of yours". I'd then have a think – who Mrs Butler was, (yet another false name). I only got paid Fridays, so I got tuppence each way, better than nothing, I s'pose.

I was nosing around at the George yard – not near the army surplus place – I gave that a wide berth. There was a wall dividing the George yard and a bombed-out school. I looked down, there was money spread around, half hidden in the rubble.

I picked up a half crown piece (2/6d), some pennies, sixpences and some threepenny pieces; all told I had found over five shillings! My lucky day.

Coming towards me were Freddy Warner and Ernie Dackham who lived in our street, which meant that they were OK. "Look you blokes" – I pointed to the wall. "I found a shilling in change under that wall", I lied. They looked around. They were big blokes, aged about 13, also wearing long trousers. One turned to the other. "Must have had a bunk-up." The other nodded: "Must have fallen out of his trouser pockets while he was having a bunk-up." "Why, was he trying to climb over the school wall with his trousers down?" I asked. I said "There was no sign of anyone who had done a poop". Their laughter increased until they were red in the face. Freddy Warner said "Did you see a 'Johnee' anywhere?" "No," I said, "I was by myself." Both blokes were falling about laughing. "Lillywhite, you're a funny kid at the best of times, but today you have made our day." They strolled off leaving me quite miffed, not knowing what had put them into such good humour. A bit later on in life I learned the meaning of bunk-up and many other words, and also that Johnny's were also called Durexes, space suits, condoms, rubbers, Johnny-bags, French letters, and more. How was I to know? Me, only eight and three quarters. I ask you.

Silver Screen

Now **there were** five cinemas locally. The Odeon, the ABC, The Golden Domes, the Grand Hall and the last and *very* least, was the Coronet, near Wells Way Canal Bridge. The first two were posh, the second two were so so, but the last one, The Coronet, defied belief.

I loved going to the cinema, so, if I had a good day's totting I'd treat myself. Once I was near to the Coronet and there was a Tom Mix western showing. I hid my barrow on some waste ground at the rear of the Coronet, brushed myself off and went in. It was cheap and I could sit anywhere. I went up to the circle; it was empty, smelly and dusty.

The film started. It was as if the man in the little room behind me was waiting for me to arrive. The film was very old and looked to me that it had been speeded up. Whilst I watched I looked around to make sure there were no Overcoat Olivers or pin droppers, as people called them, why I didn't know. I went back to watching a 100 MPH horse chase when the film broke down. Mute silence broke out. In cinemas better than this place people would shout and whistle until the film came back on. As I seemed to be alone in the place I shouted out, blew a few raspberries, then shouted Hurry up! Suddenly a light went on from the ceiling; it was the biggest light bulb I had ever seen, it showed up how grotty the place was. I heard the PROJEC-TION-ISTcoming down the steps behind me, the bare floorboards booming. He stopped, smacked me hard across my head, turned and went up to his box. Soon the film started, slowly at first, then gathering speed. The whole incident took only seconds from start to finish.

I never shouted out in a cinema again.

None of this is clockwork history. I have no concept of time, only of events, as the reader has probably surmised. I still have my barrow, and I think I am now nine years old because it's a bit easier to push when loaded.

It had been a terrible winter. As 1946 went into 1947, it was as if everything had closed down. At the end of January I was able to do some totting. I was passing Addington Square, where a lone bombed and derelict house stood on the New Church Road end. I was freezing cold, so I went in. The place was gutted. I knew from other buildings that I had been in that this house had been knocked sideways, the other houses having had a direct hit and were gone. I found some rags and a piece of zinc. One of the fireplaces looked OK and there were bits of wood and paper so with my matches I soon got a nice fire going. When I had warmed up I found a few more bits and went out to my barrow. When I returned inside the fire had collapsed outward and caught some old floorboards and some other stuff.

I quickly ran to my barrow and grabbed some old

garments that were nice and damp. I then went in and tried to put the fire out. As the roof was still on, the house was dry, making it hard going. I went out for some more rags to find a few people gathered. At that moment I heard the sound of a fire engine. More people had stopped to look. I could only think of going up before Sybil Campbell; Oh Gawd, all that I'd wanted was to get warm, and now this.

I went to go back into the house with some more wet cloths when from behind me hands held me back. "You've done enough son" said the man who was holding me. The small crowd of passers by agreed. A Green Goddess fire engine took charge and pretty soon the fire was out.

The man that had held me told the firemen that I was the hero, when he saw me trying to put the fire out. He quickly ran over to the factory opposite and they called the fire brigade.

Everyone patted me, and when someone gave me a few pennies, well they all did then. I didn't like to tell them that I had started the fire in the first place, if I would have told them they would all be in a bad mood, so why take away their pleasure?

Someone asked my name and I told them I was Harold Hawkins. Then I said, "Must go, thank you, my mum will be worried". I wheeled my barrow across Addington Square, opposite to where Westmacott Street was. Later I doubled back and went home.

Well you can't be too careful, can you?

I have only a poor recollection of having bronchial-pneumonia, as I was not conscious for quite long periods. Dr Samson, our family GP, saw me in bed and quickly phoned for an ambulance. I can remember being carried into the back of it, having no door, only a canvas curtain. I later found out that I was in Shooters Hill Hospital in an isolation wing in a very small room with one window. I was completely encased in a Perspex "greenhouse" reaching to the floor. Everyone wore masks;

it seemed like months before I could be transferred to a general children's ward.

I was told by one of the nurses that there was a boy about my age on the other side of the glass partition. We never saw each other, not even once. I did not see a human face in all that time. Hooray for the children's ward. At one end of the ward workmen were putting up tarpaper to cover up war damage. We had sing-songs from our beds – I loved this cos I could sing without stuttering; funny that. My solo piece was a song called *"Paper Doll"*; when it was my turn I would stand up on my bed in my nightshirt, always with *"Paper Doll"* to start.

One nurse in particular would cry, as her boyfriend used to sing it to her. Was he a prisoner, missing or dead? None of the other nurses would say. I still think of her crying and wonder.

After hospital I was sent away to a convalescence home in Kent, I believe near Staplehurst. I think it was for children affected by the war. Some kids hated the place. I thought it was nice, quiet; but the Matron was quite strict. I didn't mind at all. Some kids started to pinch their cheeks to try to look healthy so that they could go home. It never worked.

Working

One day, at the end of the first week I got fed-up with all the silly games – boring. The big garden fell away to a pond, past that a hut and beyond that an old gardener who I had never seen before. He ignored me. I watched while he raked up the leaves then picked out two old squares of plywood, picking up the leaves and into a wooden wheelbarrow.

I knew what I wanted to do. Before he could stop me, I picked up the old plywood squares and scooped up all the leaves into his barrow. We said nothing to each other, which gave a signal we both understood. An hour later we still hadn't spoken. When he walked down the garden to pee behind the compost heap, I tried to wheel his barrow, which only having one wheel, was awkward to balance but I moved the barrow up to where there were more leaves. He came back, raked more leaves, and stood by whilst I loaded the wheelbarrow. His arms and face were nut brown, like a pirate. "What's your name?" I told him, he turned away. "Fred", he said. I'd won, he spoke first. In the distance the bell was ringing for washing before tea. As I walked off I said "See you tomorrow". "Ah", he said. At tea the other kids were asking me where I'd been. I ignored them. They stopped when the food came around. After tea there was a games period. While the kids played, one of the staff took me to Matron's office. Fred was with the Matron, sitting on the desk. Dear me!

"Did you like gardening?" I liked doing work – so "I did enjoy working with Fred!" "You mean Mr Oakley", she snapped. "Mr Oakley" I said. Matron said "You can help with the gardening, but only what Mr. Oakley tells you, is that understood?" I nodded. Right, she said, and opened a large box full of discarded clothing – my first long trousers! A bit baggy, but a belt would hold them up. When I had fully changed, Matron beamed at me and declared I was a "real British workman". "AAR," said Fred.

I was made up.

Most days I walked down to the rear of the huge garden, we worked well and I did the stooping. Fred had a back injury from the Great War. I told him about my Grandfather being gassed at the Somme.

"AAR, Nasty" Fred said. Sometimes Fred would give me a cake. "My old Gel makes those."

"Could you please thank your old Gel for me." I was always hungry. He smiled. I went once out with Matron to Staplehurst in her little black Morris eight, a sure sign that I didn't want to escape. This was my first car ride ever.

Sunday afternoons were given to singing in the choir, Matron at the piano, and one of the staff conducting. We learned that the local people would open their doors and windows to listen – not having any wireless or newspapers this was to some their only entertainment.

How – times – have – changed.

In New Church Road there was a café wedged between the Evelina buildings and a scrap yard. The café was used by all of the totters and scrap merchants. The Colliers, the Burchmoors, the Richardsons, Joe Ludlow and many more. I decided to go in for a cup of tea, after all, I was a totter too.

I got my mug of tea and sat in an empty booth. The tables were white marble and the high forms gave some privacy. Opposite me were two men arguing, one I knew to be "Peggy" Burchmoor, who had a stump or peg leg, hence his name. The other man was getting angry and swearing. Under the table, Peggy pulled his baggy trouser leg up and carefully undid the straps of his peg, then in one graceful movement clubbed the man opposite hard over his head.

The man slumped forward into his tea whilst Peggy strapped his wooden leg back on, and calmly walked out. I drank my tea and a short while later crept out before the man woke up; I mean he might ask me if I saw anything! I crossed the café off my list.

There seemed to be gangs of kids everywhere, having war games, lobbing bricks at each other, I ask you! I was better off by myself. I had my barrow to talk to which I did sometimes; people would give me funny looks. I didn't mind. One day, in New Church Road, a gang came up behind me, kicked my barrow over and piled on me. It was like rugby scrum except I was the ball, and it was hopeless, being punched and shoved, I couldn't move. Suddenly the kid who'd started on my barrow was pinned in next to me, his shirt had come undone during the scuffle his bare shoulder next to me – so I bit him hard, not letting go. I tasted his blood as he let out a loud scream. A couple of adults walking into the road pulled the kid up now on his own; the others had scarpered. The man said "it's your own fault, go home and get it bandaged". All he said to me was "Don't bite people".

Once was enough.

One day my Dad answered a knock on the door. It was a lady from the Maudesley Hospital, who were doing a kind of survey on twins who were not identical. My twin cousins lived in the tenement opposite where we used to live. After he had explained this, my Dad said to her "Can anything be done for my son's stammer, it seems to be holding him back". She took details and soon I was an outpatient for twice a week, then also attending a speech therapist at a partly bombed school near Tower Bridge. The hospital and the speech therapy clinic took up quite a bit of school time so when some time later other kids at school in my year took the eleven-plus exams, I was sent into the yard and sat in the shed.

I don't think that I was much put out by it all, I remember being bored with nothing to do.

I finally learned to read and write. A Mr Moxon came

to our junior school with gadgets that he'd made, turning symbols into words in one term. I had got through books one, two and three. Mr Moxon took me to the headmaster's study, where I read from book three to Mr Crickmar, who beamed at me, and told me that now I would be able to read the captions in comics like the Dandy and Beano. He then gave me a threepenny piece from his waistcoat pocket. He was also very smart and had pince nez on the end of his nose. But I was still behind, hence no eleven plus.

The years went by to the sixties when a Dr Edward de Bono quantified lateral thought, its downfalls and its assets. Well done that man. No-one at school seemed to mind if I was at school or not, but you can't be in two places at once, can you?

Sundays - The Cries of London

Back in time in Westmacott Street, you would expect Sundays to be quiet; Oh No. The kids would start playing hopscotch, the older boys moving their scooters made from bomb damaged timber with ball-bearing races for wheels. Then the mothers would be out sharpening their knives on the stone steps or window sills, ready for Sunday dinner. The moment that one started, then all the women appeared, putting your teeth on edge, sounding like Robin Hood and his Merry Men fighting the Sheriff of Nottingham. Knives sharpened, they would natter, catching up on events over the last week. Pub-time.

A bit later, the women could be seen in their best pinafores with bags of vegetables going to our local pub, The Admiral Codrington (The Cod). Each woman would go into the public bar, spreading newspapers over a table. After each had bought a glass of stout, then they would pour the vegetables out onto the table, and would start peeling spuds, cutting up cabbages and all manner of other things for Sunday dinner. After a cigarette and a chat, the ladies would finish their dark beer, collect their peelings (for the chickens in the back garden), clean the tables and leave.

The menfolk by this time had washed, shaved and donned their best suits and would all meet up in the private bar for pints of "brown and mild". Jokes, cards and dominoes. Pub hours on Sunday were twelve until 2pm and four hours for evenings. So, the men would drink as many pints as they could manage before lurching homeward and sometimes falling asleep in their dinner.

I had seen this ritual many times, as I used to take my Granddad's huge jug to the pub at one o'clock on Sunday, when Joe Palsey, the publican, would fill it with "porter ale". The Coppers left the pub alone, as Joe had been a famous boxer when young; his Lonsdale belt was hung up above the bar. If there were lots of customers to be served, I would wait outside with a packet of Smith's Crisps until he could serve me. I would look at the men drinking and guess whether I would be taking their suits (if still clean) to Harvey & Thompsons next day (Monday). Probably. I was nearly always right.

Our street would be still and quiet as people ate, and then dozed in their chairs, or would go upstairs for a nap. About this time the first of the disturbances started. An old lady would push her barrow into our street, breaking the silence with a cry: 'Halt and Vinegaire". To finish off, she would ring a small bell like what teachers have in school playgrounds. On one end of her cart was a large barrel, and a wooden tap sticking out over the end of the barrow. At the other end was the biggest block of salt that you have ever seen. By the salt block there was a rusty saw tied with a long piece of tape. Also near the saw there was a large stack of newspapers. A small queue would form. Tizer bottles were popular for the vinegar, wine bottles and medicine bottles were often the cause of argument for how much they would hold, causing the nappers indoors to wake up. Shouting matches were not uncommon. The old woman dressed in a long frock, shawl and a man's cap with a huge hatpin, moved to the other end, and with the saw would cut a piece of salt off the block with the rusty saw. Each block to me looked exactly the same size as the one before, always the size of a house-brick, perfect. She would move further down the street, with cries of "Untouched by human hands" I often wondered if she washed her mits, as her fingers didn't look too clean to me.

Still, you only get what you pay for.

Just as the old woman's bell ringing faded in the distance along with shouting her wares, then there came the streetsinger who looked quite well-fed considering he was always singing about a "vagabond". His voice was deliberately awful. Every Sunday a different person would give him money, to finish his song either in Caspian Street or Picton Street, even Sears Street. He would finish combing his hair, holding his ear with his other hand and then disappear with the comb, and holding his ear seemed to be part of the act, for the comb had more teeth than the singer had hairs on his head.

That's show business for you.

The next to appear would be the Muffin and Crumpet

man, timed to sell his wares for Sunday tea; sometimes he would be beaten by the man selling shrimps and winkles, bolstering that old platitude "There is no peace for the wicked", for they both sang their wares.

In my Gran and Granddad's house Sunday was always observed. Placed before you would be one stick of celery, two slices of bread, a tomato, a quarter pint of winkles and a fish paste jar with newly ground salt and a hat pin for the winkles, all followed by a slab of cake, with a cup of tea. My Gran always put a pinch of bicarbonate of soda into the teapot, drawing out the last of the flavour. The tea when poured was almost black!

Did I mention that after the war I was sent on one convalescence in Kent and two others in Hampshire and Norfolk? Yes, I did mention it, but never mind – I can never remember in what order they were. The health authorities must have felt that I needed these holiday breaks; what with them and visits to the Maudesley Hospital and the speech clinic, they made me a stranger when I did go to school....

There was at this time a song in the hit parade called *Ch-Ch-Ch-Chew-Chewing Gum, How I Love Chewing Gum*. Soon the whole class would join in. Like a fool I would pick the nearest kid and fight him. I would, most times, be beaten up. The teacher would come into the classroom and split us up, blaming me it seemed. I must have been the most beaten up kid in the school, until I learned to laugh at my stutter as well.

Things improved at school after that. I was always running errands, things like bets to the bookie's runner. Some people would have AC-UMER-LATER bets, say six dogs in six races; if the first dog won its winnings would go onto the next dog. If they all won – "Wow". My Dad would have to work out the winnings.

He earned his fee, which could be money or food.

One errand I would do was to walk to Baldwin's, the herbalist, the last shop before the Elephant and Castle. This, when you are nine years old, is very tiring. What we would call a three day camel ride. This involved walking up to Camberwell Road, which went into the Walworth Road then right up to the railway bridge at the Elephant. I used to charge a shilling for going, with the excuse that I had to catch a bus or train. They always paid. One worried woman in our street gave me an envelope with a note and money inside, then told me to "bring the Jollop straight back to me, and don't talk to anyone!" So off I went into the Walworth Road past Westmoreland Road up to East Street, where the Sunday market is, where my mum got her bum pinched in East Street. My Dad said if a woman doesn't get her bum pinched in East Street then there must be something wrong with her. My Mum was not amused. I s'pose coming from Islington, her Dad working in Coutts Bank, she might think she was a bit above the rest of us. She used to drag me into Ikey Wright for my clothes. She being a Ladies' tailor years before, knew lots of Yiddish words that were beyond me.

When she finally bought something it was always after a verbal war, both sides thinking they had won. In the present day there is a D.J., the famous well-known character Steve Wright, who mentions his family's shop in the Walworth Road – can it be the same? I hope so.

I walked past where the pussy butcher boiled his lumps of horse up, it didn't half pong, but I finally got to Baldwin's. I gave the man the envelope. He tore it open and read. "Not again, will she ever learn?" He counted the money and went into a back room. After some time he came out with a sealed off paper bag. "Is that the bottle of Jollop?" I said. He shouted at me. "Keep your gob shut and put this in your bag and scarper". I did. Still, I earned a shilling.

That's all that counts, eh?

My Dad started to send me to the Emanuel church almost next door to Trollope & Colls that now had gone back to building, so it wasn't far. I had to go to Sunday school, evensong, early evenings and sometimes choir practice, which was a bit daft as most times there was nobody to sing to. Sunday school was taken by monks. Though the Emanuel was High Anglican, on reflection the monks teaching us looked to be of a Franciscan order. On the last day we were reading from Exodus. I will try to remember: "Moses led the Israelites from Egypt and there were 40,000 men" or words to that effect. I said to our teacher "What about the women and children? The Bible means women and children!!!" He then stood up and belted my bare knees with the knotted white rope hanging from his waist. My legs were turning mauve by the time he was finished. I stood up and walked out.

At home my Dad saw my legs, asking me what had happened. As I told him, he pulled his braces up, put his belt on and went to the church, saying nothing when he returned later. The next week I was sent on Sundays to the Salvation Army. Hallelujah!

Old Mrs Taylor died the other day; sad.

During the war she would take me in early in the morning so that my mum could go to work at Trollope & Colls, leaving my Dad to have some sleep after fire watch. She was a goodly person and was always there to help anyone. She always had the radio or wireless on. We would sit and listen to "Bing Sings" and then the free French programme, the AFN for the American servicemen over here, and the Free French programme for the homesick soldiers over here. My favourite singer was Jean Sablon who sang *"La Mer"*.

Then later came the coded messages heard after the Dot-Dot-Dot-Dash – the Victory sign giving heart to the French Resistance. When anyone died in the street, someone would hold a collection for a wreath for the deceased. Soon people will be talking about the Commonwealth, but now it was still a Common Poverty.

I learned the words to *"Paper Doll"* from the AFN (American Forces Network) in Mrs Taylor's kitchen. They weren't all bad days.

Once in a while a copper would walk his beat down our street. People would quietly disappear indoors. If there happened to be two coppers, then they were after arresting someone; some people would not come out until they were long gone.

Back in our old school, things were good. I was beginning to read quite well, considering that I had lost quite a lot of time. There was back then quite a stigma about seeing a psychiatrist. In these days it is almost fashionable; but then I was told that I would not be taking the eleven-plus exam.

Fair enough, I sat in the playground shed all that day. I seemed to be forgotten, still it was a nice day, and I joined in games with the other kids at break time.

My Dad must have done something, like he should have been consulted or told about me not sitting the exam, for I was duly given a place at Southampton Way School for Boys. Known to be a bit rough, but it wasn't too bad.

Beggars can't be choosers, and I was back in a school. As I said before, in the sixties, Dr Edward de Bono quantified lateral thinking, looking at problems, puzzles and learning from a new perspective, turning liabilities into assets. At last. Hooray!

I must have been about seven and a bit when my sister came into the world. I was made aware by our Dad telling me that I should start saving up for a new baby. I said to him "Do we really need a new baby?" After all, we had a cat that was a bit wild, but also a nice dog called Peter. I said to my Dad "had we enough room?" My Dad said that the baby had been ordered, so we would have to make space. I took a Bournville Cocoa tin, tore the paper off, made a slot in the lid and put some of my errand money in it. I often wondered what happened to it.

At Junior School I had to sit next to Pauline Gordon who lived in the Waterloo Buildings and had things crawling out of her bobbed hair, having a strong smell about her. If we were given a baby girl, I would have to make sure that she had no fleas or nits like Pauline Gordon. Anyway when the baby came everyone wanted to see it, well! the baby was covered in wrinkles and kept crying. My Aunt Doll opposite was quite envious as she had always wanted a baby girl.

I was trying to be fair, but I couldn't help thinking things like, when she is older will she be able to chop firewood and help me find shrapnel for the A.R.W. who collects it from us and loads it in his grey barrow for the war effort? The A.R.P. even cut all the iron railings from all of our old tenement buildings to help to make tanks for the invasion, as we were told.

I was staying with my Grandparents next door when my Granddad said that soon Mr Churchill, our Prime Minister, is to make an announcement on the wireless at lunchtime. I know now why Granddad was wearing his loads of medals, all clean and shiny. He stood to attention as Mr Churchill spoke. Italy had CAPIT-UL-ATED and we were no longer at war with them. When Mr Churchill had ended his speech, he stood to attention once more and saluted the wireless. He liked Italians and said they didn't want to fight us in the first place. They had many relatives living in England and America. It was all the fault of Mussolini and his fascism – whatever that meant.

On the corner of our street a man stood every day at the same time, selling dog racing results or tips. Whatever the case always standing in the same place, summer and winter, shouting his wares: "Hog Winneare!" Why do street sellers always drop the first letter of their wares? Halt & Vinegaire! As well.

I could tune our wireless into the B.B.C. Light programme, Home service and the third programme, where I could listen to good English being spoken, with beautiful rounded vowels. Two people in particular I liked to hear were a comedian called Gilly Potter, who would start off by saying "Good Evening, this is Gilly Potter speaking to you in English", and a lady called Jan de Cassarlis? who would sing funny songs for our Morale.

Most people on the wireless spoke with good voices. I suppose with me stammering, I tended to listen intently.

The only good English at one time came from the wireless – everyone that I knew spoke with a cockney twang. I was not ashamed of my accent, but it was good to hear other accents too.

Anyway, I was walking past the Dog winner man with Peter my dog, who I found one day. There were many dogs after the war, their owners killed or just abandoned, so I ended up with Peter. I found a fish barrel behind the fishmongers, carried it home in my barrow, covered over with some rags. I'm sure the fishmonger wouldn't miss one barrel less! I smuggled the barrel in through my Granddad's house, through the gate into our garden. Finding a spot for Peter's new home, turned on its side with a few bricks from the bombsite on the corner, which I propped under each side to stop it rolling. I then found a picture frame and nailed it over the front, turning the front of his barrel into a doorway. I then raised a piece of canvas over the doorway, like a curtain, put some clean rags for his bed, and hey presto, the job was done.

Peter took to his new home at once. I could hear his sniffing inside. My Mum didn't like the smell much on the dog, but after a few weeks of washing, it went away. For his housewarming, I gave him some bread and Oxo soup. He ate up whatever we gave him. Like me, he was always hungry. All my Dad said when he saw Peter and his kennel was "You found him, you feed him!" As I was good at finding things I could feed him and our cat quite well. Where was I? Oh yes, we were walking past the Dog Winner man, when Peter cocked his hind leg and peed up the man's leg. Peter didn't think that there was anything wrong. He looked too matter of fact. The man made for me, swearing non-stop. I dodged him and ran. It was said that if anyone from the Waterloo Buildings started to swear at you, they did not repeat the same word for five minutes! Well as we ran away losing ourselves over the George Yard, I could hear him using some really bad words. Now my dog is a pedigree mongrel with a dash of greyhound. I am glad to say, cos he easily outpaced me. From that day on I altered my dog-walking times. My Dad found the cat near Aldgate. He was fighting off a big dog; the dog was not winning, but the cat had lost a piece of his ear, and the tip of his tail had gone. When my Dad opened the cardboard box at home, the cat flew out, wedged himself under the legs of our gas cooker, only coming out next morning, eating something before going back under our old "Metro" gas cooker. We ignored him as he did with us. He would spit at Peter who kept his distance even when the cat attacked Peter's food bowl. We called the cat Pussy for want of a better name, but then there was a cartoon about a cat and a canary. Everyone was singing this song "I Taut I saw a Puddy Tat a Tweeping up on me". The cat with no name was now called "Puddy". Only me and my baby sister could stroke or pick Puddy up. If my Dad was out, Peter would jump into my Dad's armchair. The cat also would climb onto Dad's chair and stretch out, making the poor dog move over. There was always an uneasy peace between the two.

Sometimes the cat did not come home for weeks, then coming through the scullery door as if he hadn't been away, Puddy also would leave half of a dead mouse on the scullery doorstep, as if he was paying rent to us. Puddy would not drink still water, only drinking from a tap slightly on in the scullery.

We would have to open the scullery window so that he could stand on the sill, lean over and drink from under the tap. We just had to put up with his wild feral ways. How cold and icy were the winters then! Puddy had disappeared again for some weeks. There was a scratching on the back door. Puddy ran in, passed me through the scullery – he was covered in ice, sparkling like a Christmas tree. He ran into the warm middle room and leaped onto our red hot Kitchener stove and oven, his paws touched the cast iron top. He then screamed, turned and ran back out into the pitch black garden and beyond. Not even a few seconds had passed from beginning to end.

Puddy came back after a few weeks, his paws almost healed, as if nothing had happened, and started on Peter's dinner. All the other dogs in Westmacott Street were also a bit scared of him, looking the other way if he was sometimes walking with me. All except a small dog called Spot who was mostly Jack Russell. He was the best ratter you could have. If he heard the word Rats, he would snarl and salivate. My Aunt Doll lived opposite the Borketts where Spot lived; someone shouted "Rats", Spot vaulted across the street, into Aunt Doll's ground floor tenement and came out with a huge rat. Ratty Jarvis beware, Spot was on the job!

My thinking was that with the intense bombing during the war had changed not only people but also the mouse and rat population. They too were unsettled! My Mother had placed our week's bacon ration of four slices per family in the scullery. Puddy, as feral as ever, jumped through the window and grabbed the bacon in his mouth and ran up the garden and climbed up a tree, with my Mum in hot pursuit, and watched our cat eating the lot, unable to do anything about it. My Mother's face was a picture of hate. The cat stayed away for weeks: "To the Victor, the Spoils".

My Granddad had made rattrap cages and caught many, using his skills in catching rats in the trenches during the First World War. He would drown them in an old bath tub, then when dead would burn them on the fire made from wood that I would bring from local bomb sites. Thus we kept the rat population down. My Grandmother was, when young, a Dover girl and spoke with a Kentish burr. She was only five foot two high and was blind in one eye, and her looks were not much to be desired. She was always making potions, medicines, ointments; remedies for everything. She was very lucky; had she been born in the middle ages, she may have been burned as a witch, who knows? My Grandfather, on the other hand, was extremely good looking, six feet eight and a half, ramrod straight back. His boots were size 13 ½, he had spent twelve years in the Royal Artillery and eight years in the Royal Marines. He loved his King and Country. He was the personification of Great Britain and its Empire. Woe betide anyone who said anything against – sparks would fly. I think that my Granddad fell in love with my Gran's cooking, wisely ignoring her looks – she could make a meal out of anything. Looking back, I dread to think what I ate. It would be best not knowing what her herbs and spices could do – it was best not knowing the contents.

Most people kept rabbits and chickens in their gardens as part of the food chain. Trouble was, they became attached to them and were reluctant to slaughter them. That's where my Granddad came in. He would do the job that they could not do. He would gently hold an old hen, stroke her calming the old bird, then with his large index finger and thumb either side of the hen's gullet and snap his finger and thumb. It was over. He did the same with rabbits – a quick and painless ending. He would then bleed the animal, then skin or pluck it clean and prepare the animal for cooking, charging sixpence or a shilling.

He was kept fairly busy.

Granddad was also a wood carver, probably learned to carve in the trenches of the Great War. He made me a dancing man about 12 inches high with articulated arms and legs. He would insert some thick wire into the back of the dancing man, about a foot long, wind up his old gramophone, the record that he always played was *"Whisper it why you'll never leave me"* As the record turned, he would gently bounce the dancing man, barely touching the record. It was magic! Kids in the street would ask to see the dancing man performing in Gran and Granddad's parlour.

How he could carve these dolls, to me was quite amazing, all made with an old penknife. I'll talk more of him later.

Double Bedlam

The first time that I went alone to the Maudesley Hospital was almost my last. I went into the children's wing in a side road. As I entered, a huge man in a white jacket stepped out from nowhere and pinned my arms behind my back and frog-marched me up to a desk. A lady behind the desk said sharply "You can let him go! He is not violent, are you?" He smiled. "N-N-No; Ma'am" I stuttered. She pointed to a door, after I gave my name. Knock and go in. I thanked her. For the hour, the doctor asked me lots of silly questions, he then took me to another room where there was a group of boys about my age, all sitting around with another doctor in the centre. Sitting next to a boy of my age who looked normal. I was wrong.

He glared at me and pulled out a tin the shape of a snuffbox, and quickly rolled a cigarette, lit it and puffed away. No one took any notice. He grinned, saying he was allowed to smoke as it helped his nerves. He joined in the general conversation. Another kid couldn't stop sniffing; one of the others was making animal noises. The doctor kept the chatter going, it was very free and easy. I said to one kid who also looked normal, "Why are you here?" "Most times" he said, "I am quite OK, but when I am out, I can't stop picking up cats and throwing them up in the air"

"How high can you throw them?" said I, trying to think what to say. "About a yard", he said and smiled. "Course", he said, "they always land on their feet", as if that made it OK. Opposite me, sat a kid that I immediately Christened Lord Snooty from the comics, Dandy and Beano. He had taken off his tweed, double-breasted overcoat, showing him in his school uniform (well tailored), a white shirt and good shoes. When I had finished staring at him, he shouted "how do you do:" I tried to copy his greeting, but failed on the second syllable. "Where do you live?" said the kid who'd been smoking. "Other side of Camberwell Green" I said. "Yuk" one had said. "We live in Sussex", Lord Snooty said. As none of us knew where Sussex was, he was ignored.

One sunny afternoon, our doctor decided we would have a game of rounders. There were about eight of us, so in the centre of the hospital where the three sides met was a triangle of grass. Ideal. I had hit the ball when it was my turn to bat, but now I was fielding; the bowler kept changing his stance and practising his throws for too long! The kids were getting impatient. Suddenly the batter could stand no more. He threw the bat at the bowler with such force, hitting the bowler square on his forehead, knocking him to the ground, out cold. If you had blinked, you could have missed the whole scenario. Everyone raced to pick up the kid who was down, leaving the batter staring into space. It was the first and last rounders game.

At the end of the session at Maudesley I walked up to

Ruskin Park. There were still ramparts of a big house. Past that was a folly in the shape of a summerhouse. I would sit inside looking over a lake and flowerbeds. I would unwind, wondering where this was going to end. Once the park keeper wanted to know why I wasn't at school. When I told him that I was under the "Maudesley", he couldn't get away quick enough. I had just turned my liabilities into assets. A few weeks later, back in the Maudesley, Lord Snooty approached me when the session came to an end. "I say, would you care to go to the pictures?" I said that I had no money. "That's all right, I'll pay, I have money over from my allowance". We were lucky to get pocket money; he had an allowance. How the rich live.

I told him of the film at the "Golden Domes" called "London's Pride", a kind of musical. He agreed. Outside, a man with a huge car was waiting and off we went, sitting in the rear. He gave the instruction to the driver and in no time we were there. The car had a small shield printed on the side. Whilst the driver looked at the time when the film would be over, Lord Snooty suddenly went next door to the bakery and bought a small cottage loaf, leaving me to wonder why. A servant at home should have bought it – strange.

The film had just started, it was in Technicolor, which was great. I was spellbound. Sometime later I happened to look at Lord Snooty. He was stuffing great chunks of bread into his mouth like an animal. Pieces were flying everywhere. He finally stopped eating, offering me some. Disgusted, I refused. He said "Every so often in our family tree someone is born eccentric. I'm afraid it's me this time" and started to laugh. I swear that his eyes glared in the dark. I made my way to the lavatory, spotting the driver sitting in the back row watching Lord Snooty. I crept out of the cinema and walked home, thinking Lord Snooty may be eccentric, but where I come from he would be thought of as mad.

As I walked home after seeing only half of the film, I thought of Lord Snooty. Perhaps he was lonely, with no friends, with all that money and no one to be mates with. Whereas I have a good Mum and Dad, and a sister who is growing up nice and there was Peter and Puddy our mad cat. I'm glad that we're not posh.

I never saw him again – maybe he was moved nearer to where he lived.

Alma Mater 2

Time hopping again – my first day at Secondary School, as I went through the gate, I was hit in full face by a sucked-out orange. I kept walking and was directed into the headmaster's study. I knocked. "enter". I went in. Mr Coombs stood up, reaching for his cane. "Right George, put your hand out, I haven't got all day, you've had this coming to you for ages". "Excuse me, sir, this is my first day" I quietly said (I had no time to stutter) and I kept looking at his enormous cane. "Was there another boy out there?" he said. "No sir". "Well pop out and look for George". I did, and there was. George went in. I heard a few thwacks before he reappeared, rubbing his hand. Meanwhile, Mr Coombs looked me up on his chart. "You are in One B". The kid then said "I'm to take you to your class, 1B". "He kept calling me George", I said. "He calls everyone George" the kid said, "even the teachers". "Why?" "'Cos he's insane" he said. He then explained to me that 1B was average, 1A were bright kids and 1C were idiots. I was delighted being average, I had never been average at anything, and now I was where I wanted to be. Even better were my winter term results: I was sixteenth in a class of thirty-two. Average!

Mr Young, our form teacher, pointed to the back of the classroom. "Sit there". In front of me, two down, sat Stanley

Crane, in front of him was a kid called Emmet, from Junior School. No one in our class seemed to be taking any notice of Mr Young, who seemed to be talking to himself.

Sometimes he would shout "Pay attention!" which only caused a short lapse in conversation. It suited me sitting at the back, and I had no one behind to annoy me, bliss.

Some teachers were really good. Mr Bleyney, Maths; strict. Mr Benjamin, English; sense of humour, good at teaching drama. Mr Astill, Art; had a cruel tongue.

There came one day to our school, a lady with a cello. In assembly we were briefed, there was going to be a recital at 11a.m. that day. Our school was musically motivated in every way, except for the orchestra, who could play not one note in tune, or at the same time. It has been said that some people grow to resemble their pets, and vice versa. The lady cellist did look like her given instrument, being slightly bottom heavy, with a diminished waistline, and some other unmentionable features.

She sat over her cello, showing us her well-nourished knees and played beautifully, egged on by some younger kids, who, every time she played a musical rest, would applaud wildly, hoping the concert was finally over, incurring glaring looks from their form masters. Finally she ended her three set cello pieces.

I cannot quite remember them in detail, but in my head it was Bach's No. 1 Cello Suite, a piece of Elgar's Cello and Saint Saens' Swan from The Carnival of the Animals.

Perhaps I would have liked these pieces to be played in retrospect; I do not know, so I shall settle for what I wrote.

Back in time, still at school, a music teacher would appear. I never did hear him speak to anyone. He played the old Broadwood piano at break times and assembly. He rejoiced in the name of Mr/Dr Titchyarty. Most of the time he would be locked away with the orchestra at the far end of the school. He, to complete the picture, wore "bombay bloomers" summer and winter, not doing general appearance much good, as he was very short and quite fat for that post-war period.

Sometimes it was possible to hear braying sounds, say, of a wounded elephant or suchlike. My theory being that Mr Coombs, our insane headmaster, had press-ganged all the outcasts, nutters and no-hopers into the orchestra where they could be kept at bay. The cacophony became awful as I neared, putting crates of empty milk bottles to be collected next day – Eddy and I were still milk monitors.

The leader of the orchestra, by self appointment, was one Chrissy Istead. He walked around the school taking his viola into geography, English, history – all classes, even football practice, everywhere. New scholars of all ages were warned 'Not to joke" about Chrissy Istead's viola, as he was known to be "tasty" in a fight. Also, he kept the other musicians, specially the nutters, under control. In later years I saw an American film called "The Valentine's Day Massacre" in which the shooters carried their guns in violin cases, which so much reminded me of Chrissy Istead lugging his viola everywhere.

I must confess that not once did I ever see his viola; it was as if he was jealous of any attention paid to it. Ah well.

Out of the blue, a black man came to our school to become our teacher. His subject was technical drawing. It turned out he was an exchange teacher from America. The poor unsuspecting man, to come all the way from the U.S.A! Surely the authorities could find him a better school than ours? I mean to say! I'd read in my Dad's paper something about Joe Dimmagio, a famous baseball player, so I thought when he had settled in, I would ask our new teacher about him. Meanwhile, he had looked in our stationery cupboard. It was empty, no pencils, paper, rulers, in short nothing. Mr X, on the other hand, had foraged around, finding enough to carry on with until the weekend. Come Monday morning, we filed into our classroom to find every desk was equipped with new pens, rulers, pencils, erasers, compasses, the lot. Mr X (his name escapes me) had worked miracles. But next morning, most of the equipment had gone. Mr X did not go into a rage, but instead told us that he had spent most of his weekend buying our new stores from his own pocket. He was a bit upset. We were very quiet that day and treated him with politeness and respect. Next day most of what he had bought came back, which put a smile on his face. Soon after, we kind of bonded with our teacher. Most of us had never been this close to a black person, let alone a teacher.

One day I told him what I knew about Joe Dimmagio and baseball. Mr X demonstrated how a pitcher threw the ball, standing on one leg, twisting his body slightly, his right hand poised to throw the ball. The class door opened and in came Mr Coombs, looking through our teacher – then caning two boys, leaving one bemused teacher as he walked out.

We all explained to Mr X what went on most mornings. What happened next was that our teacher left suddenly. None of us knew why – his legacy to us was a good stock of drawing equipment. We all missed him.

This gap was filled by another new teacher, not staying long enough to remember his name, but could he sing! The man was short, stubby and barrel chested. He had a basso profundo voice. Every morning before lessons he would sing an aria, firstly taking his tuning fork from his top-pocket. His singing resounded round the room, so powerful was his voice.

Most of the class enjoyed his songs and bits of opera, though none would say, until one morning after the "drinking song" Donald Windsor blew out a raspberry. The singing teacher said "I shall never sing again" and he didn't, leaving most of us all the poorer now that his singing was no more. Shame.

In my third year at school, we took delivery of a Panphonic sound system, built in modules, it was the last word in sound quality, at the time the nearest thing to stereophonic sound. We were the first school to receive one. What a waste! When the euphoria was over the system was installed in the "orchestral room". Two or three times a week at lunch-break time certain teachers would play their records to us third and fourth years. Surprisingly, these became popular, some blokes used the record concert as a midday flop house, much to the annoyance of Mr Coombs, who would enter and prod anyone with closed eyes, shouting "Wake up George!"

Most teachers brought their own records – no mean feat considering a Beethoven symphony weighed an awful lot. The wax records, six per symphony, would fill a medium suitcase. Vinyl came later. So our teachers' efforts were spoiled by Mr Coombs' antics, which caused many a black look when he would finally leave from all in the classroom.

Thinking of the Cello years later, of our cello lady straddling her instrument, clamping it tight with her knees, and then comparing it, say, with Paul Tortelier, the French world famous cellist and the modern day wonder Yo Yo Ma; who have both perfected the technique of using a long spike, lying back relaxed, supine, their cellos gently leaning on them as one. No stress or discomfort, just absolute good playing, good music, good to watch, plus its musical range and sound are very much akin to the human voice. God bless the Cello.

Do As You Would Be Done By

I think it was the late forties when the accident happened. Our class had its own bully named Brian Hillier, who early in his puberty had outgrown us all.

When Mr Young needed a cigarette break to calm his nerves, he would be away for eight to ten minutes.

Our bully would walk up each aisle smacking, pinching, punching, hair-pulling, whatever. He came to our aisle. His first stop was Emmet, flicking poor Emmet's bat-wing ears until they were black and blue. Next was Stanley Crane's turn. Brian the bully would gently pat his plump cheeks, hitting harder and harder until they were very red. Next it was my turn. I tried to ignore him as he stood and grabbed my hair at my temple, twisting, causing much pain. I'd had enough. When he finally let go, I sprang up off my form, bringing my fist upwards at the same time with such force that he fell back onto those old fashioned iron radiators fixed on the wall behind where I sat. He fell to the floor and didn't move. Mr Young came in, looked and told a boy to fetch the Headmaster, and to call for an ambulance. I was taken to the Headmaster's study, passing the Headmaster on the way. I was asked questions by the School secretary, who was sympathetic. Later came the police. By this time I was blubbing, crying like a baby, thinking that Brian Hillier was dead. I was reassured that he had regained consciousness, but would not probably come back to the school. I heard a lot later that Brian had a plate in his head where his skull had hit the radiator and was now at a different school. I found out later that the police had interviewed the whole class one at a time, finding out his bullying ways from his victims. Much to my relief, the whole incident passed off and was soon forgotten. Only a few of the kids spoke to me after that. I also think it helped me being under the Maudesley only up at Denmark Hill.

Most people had the wrong impression of it, thinking it to be some form of a lunatic asylum.

In my third year at school, I wanted to visit the commercial show at Earls Court. My then teacher said "No, Lillywhite, we hardly see you here at school as it is. Earls Court is out of the question" All that I had to say was "My Psychiatrist thought that it would be good for me". He could not write me out a chitty for the Earls Court Commercial Motor Show quick enough. Easy!

Earlier on at school some in our class were going into the mainstream learning French. I idly wondered if I would stutter speaking another language. This idea was cut short by the same teacher, who said, to quote: "It's pointless, Lillywhite, you can't even speak English properly". We are talking 1950s here; people still were frightened of any aspect of mental health.

Back to the late "forties". Due to my Dad's efforts, I

was seen by another doctor, and started speech therapy in Bermondsey, near Tower Bridge. We were a mixed bag of all ages, our therapist/teacher was a Miss Lloyd. She wore "ladies" clothes, a little out of date, but you could see that she was from a different world. She would start with a group "chat" on any topic, followed by lip exercises. During the session we would have a relaxing period. Each of us would go to the cupboard and take a pillow and a sheepskin rug. We would lie supine, hands by our sides waiting to relax. We didn't. Miss Lloyd would have an intake of students now and then, who came among us, bending over, lifting our arms up to see if we were properly relaxed – not such a good idea with blokes just going through pubescence. A mixture of perfume and Lifebuoy soup, then tight-fitting blouses on a sunny day, was all it took. On seeing an erection on her charge, she would quickly move on to the next bloke. No one had any chance of relaxing that day.

One kid, too young for this malarkey, was clearly tensed up; the young student saying "Relax" over and over to the distraught kid. In the end he said "OK, Miss". He relaxed and the loudest fart in Bermondsey could be heard. It brought the house down. Not everything was as funny as this.

Once every month a visiting psychiatrist would see us one at a time in a consulting room along the corridor. Yes, you might have guessed it, he was a bum-fondler, who liked smaller kids in short trousers. Nothing was ever said, even

– 64 –

if reported, no one seeming to be bothered in those days. Miss Lloyd could never understand how our speech defects were always worse when he was around.

Sometimes after speech therapy, four or five of us would catch the same bus. It could be hilarious upstairs on the bus; we would review the day's proceedings. Martin, who lived near East Street could only talk after he had expended every breath of air from his lungs. He would be, by this time, red in the face. He would now croak: "LETSGETOFFNEXTSTOPANDBUYSOMEDOUGHNUTS". He would now take a deep breath before he passed out! Another kid could only talk when he hit his right side hip. When getting the rhythm right after a few hits, he could then say: "I-Have-No-Bleeding-Money". When he stopped hitting himself it signalled the end of his conversation in March time. This other kid sounded like a sheep – "I'LL-P-A-A-A-Y", reminding me of Larry the Lamb in Toytown on the wireless. Then I joined in, screwing my face up and going pop-eyed to complete the picture.

It was a sight to behold the look of other passengers on the bus, which was embarrassed shock horror – poor people. Earlier at the speech therapy, Miss Lloyd would get us in a rough circle, one boy would march round our chairs saying "I am the first link", then the remaining boys would bellow "OF THE CHAIN OF GETTING BETTER". This way, everyone had a turn, no-one stammered. Ok. This was all well and good, but you couldn't when talking to all and sundry, walking in circles, telling bewildered people that you were the third link "of the chain of getting better" could you? Sometimes we were joined by an older bloke who grunted like a pig – a kind of honking sound – just to complete the picture. Whatever anyone else thought, we as a group would always laugh at ourselves.

I heard later that the bloke who thumped his hip was now having treatment, as his hip was growing distorted. Sad.

Sometimes, after a session at the speech therapy clinic, I stroll down Tower Bridge Road, past Sarsons Vinegar factory, past the Leathermakers College, further on to Pickfords Lorry depot, then to the Trocette cinema. On the far side of the road was a bakery called Edwards who cooked doughnuts in the window for a penny each – I can still taste them!

Behind the Trocette; bomb debris had been cleared and tarmacked, a market was being installed. Not just fruit and veg., but Antiques. I walked there regularly and started to run errands for the stallholders, eventually minding their stalls whilst they went for a pee or a coffee. The market was expanding. It was named the New Caledonian Market, possibly after an old market in Islington.

I made myself useful with the dealers going from one to the other. They were a friendly lot, seeming all to have Humber Pullman. cars with wooden coach-built backs. I got treated well by them as I was useful. One of my regulars asked me to mind his stall, having business with another dealer.

An American lady came over to our stall, her eyes focussed on a powder horn made of wood, brass, horn and ivory. I said "all I can tell Ma'am is that it is early Georgian. Mr P., the dealer, is teaching me the trade when I finish at my speech school", I lied. She opened the ivory bung and squinted inside. "Gee, that's dirty" she said, looking at the mock spider's web that old sulphur and black gunpowder makes. She smiled. "Sure does stink", she pulled a face. I said with my best stammer "That's because it's genuine and authentic" The price said three guineas. "How much is that", she said. "Three pounds and three shillings Ma'am". I counted the money from her palm. "I shall dine out on this story back home". She left smiling. When the dealer came back, I gave him the money for the horn. He went mad, telling me no-one would look at it. "You must have a good sales patter`", and paid me extra!!!

If things went quiet, I would have a look round at the other side, the general market. This side was vibrant and noisy, stall-holders shouting their wares, doing demonstrations, as part of the entertainment One man holding up chinaware would shout *"All cheap and cheerful ladies, all guaranteed!"* "How long for?" someone shouted back. *"No no no, lady – guaranteed stolen!!!"* The crowd would buy some after having a good laugh. The best "spieler" of all sold a potion, elixir, whatever, that would kill any fleas, lice, bedbugs, silverfish, wasps, nits and cockroaches. "The contents of this bottle will rid your house of those unwanted pests". He would open a box and bring out a handful of assorted bugs and insects, laying them on a piece of plate glass; he would pour a drop of the killer potion over them. Instantly, the insects would roll over and die. "To prove how safe it is for mammals and such like, I will now drink some myself". He would then, with a great sense of theatre, gulp some down from the same bottle that had killed the bugs and insects. He sold out by the time the market was over. I knew there was a catch – I'd solved the racket in a few days. Inside the pub, waiting for my Grandparents' jug of porter ale I noticed a fly over the counter walk into some spilt beer. When the fly walked away it staggered all over the counter before it could take off. That was it. He probably bought coloured essence from Baldwins' shop at the Elephant and Castle. He didn't kill the insects off, instead he got them drunk! Adding a spot of whisky and beer to each brew, by the end of his working day, he himself was probably pie-eyed too.

Those poor, hung-over insects were most likely used again when they came too

Not really a job for the RSPCA.

By now, the spieler is probably C.E.O. to a major drugs company. Who knows?

Back to the end of the War in Europe, it had ceased. People were now stripping the brown strips of paper from windows, collecting their belongings from air-raid shelters, ridding their houses of awful black-out curtains – Hooray!

Camberwell Green market had come back to life, though not much to sell. An old man had put up beside the fishmonger. He had found an old bassinette pram, removed the hood and nailed an old bombsite cupboard door over the length of the pram, covering it over with a faded Union Jack so that it draped over the sides. On the flag stood an ancient gramophone with a large horn facing outward. By the side was a stack of old 78 R.P.M. patriotic wax records. I can still hear "Rule Britannia" and "There'll always be an England". His old cap soon filled up with pennies and ha'pennies. All he had to do was keep winding the gramophone up and change the needle and empty his cap, showing his medals from the Great War. Good luck to him.

On the other side of the road, among the debris sat the cat lady on her fold-up stool, about to feed the stray cats. They knew what time to congregate. She had picked up yesterday's plates licked clean – never needed to be washed. Sometimes, the fishmonger threw over pieces of fish "on the turn" to the affray. She never acknowledged him or anyone else. People would throw rusty tins of food (hoarded during the war having seen better days) her way. The only time that she ever spoke was to the cats. I used to think that she lived at the Ladies' Doss House on the way to Walworth called Saint Jemma's. The house was located on the cross road where the Albany Road started, dividing Walworth from Camberwell.

If you ever passed St. Jemma's, you had to be careful; an inmate would spring out onto the pavement. Their cry would be "Can you see me over the road please?" All St Jemma's ladies sound like parrots, could be that they have not one tooth between them. But they seemed to enjoy the game of Road Crossing, when arriving at the Albany Road side, they sat on the bench in the small green area, waiting for someone to see them back. In later years I often wondered if their little game was the only point of human contact outside Saint Jemma's hostel that they ever had. Shame that I didn't realise this at the time. Idiot.

Crossing over onto the Walworth Road, there was Clubland, a kind of youth club and a charity supported by lots of people; film stars and radio personalities. Shortly after the war had ended, Bob Hope paid a visit to Clubland. On a makeshift stage, he treated us all to some of his jokes, wearing a large cowboy's ten gallon hat, also singing "Thanks for the Memory". The crowd loved him. It was said that he was born in Eltham near Kent before seeking his fortune in America. In his way, by doing a lot of entertaining of the allied troops fighting the Germans, (also we could always hear him on A.F.N.) keeping our spirits up. Whilst entertaining us, he had caused a traffic jam. No one seemed to mind.

Danger UXB

I haven't told you about a bomb that I found – yes, but it was quite small. I was looking over a bombsite, finding things. I turned over a piece of wood and there it was. The bomb had split open and white powder had leaked out. It had been raining so over the time, the powder had turned to liquid. Where the bomb had split, I could see that this bomb was made of tin.

No wonder the Germans had lost the war! Cheapskates! A tin bomb, painted grey, about one and a half feet long with fins at one end. I knew what to do.

During the war, when it was safe to go to the pictures, and when the cinemas were showing some Disney cartoons, in between cartoons we watched Government films, things like using a gas mask. The man who was always the same person, whose name was Freddy Grisewood, was also a B.B.C. announcer. He always wore a dinner suit and a tin helmet. One film was about finding bombs or land-mines, telling us all not to touch them and quickly call the A.R.P, or the police or the fire brigade (as it was then). I hurried back to Westmacott Street and ran into Hardy's General store. He had been in charge of the local section of the A.R.P., as he was the only one with a telephone. Although the war was well over, he would know what to do. I gave him a description – where it was – and told him that some other boys had told me. After all, I didn't want the coppers asking me what was I doing in the first place. Mr Hardy jumped at the idea that heard about the U.X.B. as he called it. When the bomb disposal men from the army had departed, Mr Hardy told me that it was an UN-EXPLOD-ED IN-SEND-IARY bomb and was quite dangerous.

He gave me a toffee.

My Aunt Clare and Uncle George came over from Canada for a holiday on the Queen Mary liner!

Earlier they had passed their geology course, and a firm of prospectors had financed them with a Landrover to go into the interior of Canada to look for gold.

Because they were given a British vehicle, my uncle dressed himself in tweeds and a deerstalker hat, shouting "Tally ho" to passers by, putting on a posh British accent. Everything to him was a joke. They were two of a kind. With all the surveying equipment at hand, they found no gold, alas, instead they found oil! Later they sold their share to an oil company, making them quite well off for the time being, so they toured the U.S.A. We met them at Waterloo Station; it was great. I was about eleven years old, and could remember seeing my cousins off years before on wartime evacuation, hundreds of kids on the platform waiting for the train to take them from London's bombing.

I wasn't to go, my mum saying back then that if we should die in the bombing that we would die together.

She seemed to think this was noble. Suddenly one boy started crying, his ticket pinned to his coat falling off. That started a chain reaction. Within a short time all the kids were in tears. I was more interested in the steam locomotive, wishing I could ride on the train. Ah well.

My Uncle George and Aunt Clare met during the last war. My Aunt's first husband threw himself under a tube train earlier, troubled by the forthcoming war, his religious conviction, and the break-up of his marriage. My aunt was devastated, my mum said, until she met George, who restored the world of love, kindness and tolerance, which stayed with them for the rest of their lives.

I was enthralled for the first time when I met him at my other Grandmother's house in Islington. He was a master sergeant in the Canadian army and was waiting to go over to France, wearing a strange battle dress, the like of which I had not ever seen before. He also had to carry his Sten gun with him in readiness. When I asked, he let me hold his Sten gun – it was so heavy that I nearly dropped it! He also had the biggest vacuum flask I had ever seen. He told me, with his soft accent, that "we get mighty cold when flying" so he and his troop drank coffee" to keep us warm". Shortly after this time he went to war. My hero. Fortunately for all of us, he came back; many didn't.

They eventually made a life in Canada doing all sorts of wondrous things in their lives together, often sending us toys and food, their parcels eagerly awaited. Everyone should have an Aunt Clare and an Uncle George.

At one time we received a parcel with a cap gun for me and kids' books for my sister who was growing up fast. The little books in a hard folder, were all about a magic place called Dipsy Doodle. I am sure these little books were the cause of Barbara reading so early. When she was old enough for a pushchair, my mum wanted me to push her round the streets. What would people say? I would lose my status of running errands for people in the street and going out totting and finding things, so I would make myself scarce.

She (my sister) was always asking "what's this word?" or "what does this word mean?". I was barely able to read myself at my age. From an early age I could see that she was bright at school and would go far with an education. Grammar school came next, her doing so well that Miss Gibbs, the Headmistress, called my mother to the school, telling my mum that Barbara had worked hard and deserved a place at Oxbridge. People of our kind only attended red brick universities, if lucky. Miss Gibbs also stated the school had private funds in the shape of extra grants, but my mother talked my sister Barbara out of university completely by pleading poverty – which was not true. Ah well, lackaday.

Back to the roaring forties. In Lomond Grove there stood a water tank for fire fighting during the war, now used by kids for swimming. The water had gone green. At this time there were outbreaks of poliomyelitis and infantile paralysis. Someone had written to the newspapers, blaming the water tanks. They were soon taken down.

Westmacott Street was back to normal. The trucks going into Pye Transport in Southampton Way were using our street as a "rat run" laden with stinking cowhides destined for the tannery.

In my school holiday, I would jump onto a forty-two bus to Aldgate where my dad now had two jobs, one with the Cleansing Department in the City of London, the other was running a busy paper stall opposite Aldgate tube station, in a large tailor's shop front called Max Cohen. My Dad worked for Ike selling Newspapers. Ike seemed to be into everything. By the time "Max Cohen" opened his shop at nine a.m., Dad's paper stall had gone, cleaned and swept.

I would help when my Dad got very busy about 7.45 am. Sometimes we would run out of papers. I would run over to the other stall for him. Ike and I would run over, loaded with newspapers for my Dad. Ike had a brand new car, a Morris. He gave us a lift in it once around the City – that made three cars I had ridden in!

There were so many newspapers at the time, the Daily Herald, the News Chronicle, the Daily Star, the Standard and many more, gone for good, making life easier for newspaper sellers. One crowded, busy time I was helping my Dad serve a lady asking for a News Chronicle. I misheard and gave her the Jewish Chronicle instead. The lady went berserk at me, using bad language. My Dad appeased her by giving her a News Chronicle free. She went off. I said "You have possibly lost a customer over my mistake". He said "people like her we can do without anyway".

Here I go, flitting through time again, whizzing the hands of my clock back through time, to my lovely day out at Earls Court Commercial Motor Show. Having now a pass to go, I showed it to my Dad, who planned a route by bus and tube train. He made me memorise each stop and station. When the day came, I was up early washed and changed, made my sister's porridge, left her with my gran next door and now I was off!

After changing buses and tubes I arrived at Earls Court, only a short walk from the underground. There it was; I was flabbergasted. Earls Court was enormous – the biggest building I had ever seen. Inside it took my breath away. There were makes of lorries and trucks being dwarfed inside this huge building. Names were known to me like Ford, Leyland, Atkinson, Erf, Foden, Scammel, Trojan, Ferguson and many more, and there were lots of stalls and stands, some having trays of food, things on sticks and lots of drinks. No one seemed to take any notice of me, which was great. I was easily the youngest there. After climbing in and out of so many vehicles, I spotted a "free enterprise" stand. They had a large muslin carrier bag to give away. I had put on my most polite accent with lots of "excuse me" and "pardon me", "please may I", which kept me quite well fed. A few people asked why I was not at school. I would show them my school pass. It was written on paper with our new name – Dovedale Manor. (Schools like ours changed their names and turned over a new leaf. It didn't work!) With my new carrier bag, I collected brochures of every lorry, eating at all stands that had food and drink – it was great. The vast sound system came alive. "There will shortly be showing a promotional film in the cinema". I made sure I had a good seat. Whilst waiting for the film, its loudspeakers played Elgar's Pomp and Circumstance march – Land of Hope and Glory. The film was all about British Achievement at all levels! Good stuff. I went round again in case I had missed anything, hoovering up any discarded items or leftovers before going home before the rush-hour started. This had been the best day of my life!

My form master was taken with the Free Enterprise bag with all the brochures in it; some did the rounds, ending up in many classrooms, brightening the place up a bit. It was amazing what could be done with the mention of a psychiatrist, turning liabilities into assets.

Looking back on my school days in a better light, it really wasn't that bad. Recently talking to people that went to other schools, I am sometimes in shock at some of the things they say and how they think. I mean, once you got used to Mr Coombs doing his mid-morning walk along the corridor swishing his cane like d'Artagnan in The Three Musketeers. He had got into the habit of going into a classroom unannounced, ignoring the form master, pointing to a boy – "Stand up George", and the boy knew what was coming – thwack! Mr Coombs would turn away towards the next classroom, leaving the last teacher looking bemused, meanwhile "George" in the next class would wonder "why me?", and so it went on. There were certain teachers he would leave alone, they were "old school" and strict. He only violated newer teachers, who didn't seem to last long.

One instance at school was pretty bad. A pupil whose surname was Archibald, was something of a sad sack. I remember a new teacher getting angry with Archibald and throwing the poor kid into a corner of the classroom. After a while, Archibald got up and ran home, just as his father, a Dustman, met him, and heard the sad story. He rushed to the school, called the teacher out, a fight ensued. A fourth form pupil called Scullion grabbed both men and held them apart until they calmed down. Scullion was six feet two inches tall and weighed thirteen stone, all muscle and still growing. No-one messed with him. The matter was closed.

Most of the teachers were, by and large, good, making what they could out of a bad job. One teacher was Mr Benjamin, who took us for English Lit. and would not stand for any nonsense. His lessons covered poetry, plays, drama and composition. He always had a lively class at break time or sometimes lunch time he would spend ten minutes of his time helping me with my stammer. "Now Lillywhite, I have noticed that you stammer on certain letters and not on others. The thing is, you will probably stammer for most of your life". I nodded. "The trick is to first learn to live with what you have. Our language is very rich and diverse; therefore by increasing your vocabulary, it will enable you to use other words and phrases to help you along. Are you willing to try?" Again I nodded, so that was what we did.

I think that I had more success with Mr Benjamin and his odd ten minutes' tuition than all that the Maudesley Hospital put together with speech therapy to boot! I progressed. One day, he gave me a Bible, saying "Open it at any page and read it aloud from the top of the page". I stumbled at first but picked up as I went along. "Good show" he said. We went on to vocabulary – more new words and phrases. He came to be my critic, my mentor and my friend.

The day came for me to read the lesson at Assembly after prayers. Mr Benjamin picked out a suitable passage which I read a few times.

I was called on to do my bit by Mr Coombs. I faced the whole school, plus teachers. I started, after reading a few lines with a few pauses. I got stuck in, my confidence growing halfway through, reading faster. Then faster. "Slow down George" said the Headmaster. I did, and soon it was over. I closed the Bible. "Well done George". Praise indeed from the cane waving d'Artagnan. I was never asked again, partly because my cousin Peter did the Bible reading, as he was the "Head Boy" and a year older.

Some blokes, knowing of Mr Benjamin's efforts, called me teacher's pet – not in a bad way, just having a laugh.

Since my earlier debacle with Hillier, the school bully, I was pretty much left alone, which made life easier. I had made a few friends by then.

Donald Windsor was the most caned bloke in the school. If there was any trouble in the class, he was in it. We were always losing teachers; they would last for a few weeks and resign, leaving the hard core of seasoned teachers to cope, until another unsuspecting teacher arrived. Windsor was on form. The new teacher sent for the cane and record book from the headmaster's study. The normal cane was about two feet six inches long, unlike Mr Coomb's birch cane measuring about five feet long. The teacher then caned Don with a great sense of theatre. As he filled in the cane record book, stooping over his desk table, Don took a few paces back, then ran at the teacher's rear end, kicking the gullible teacher up his "daily mail". The poor teacher was now lying with his upper torso prone on his own desk in some discomfort. Meanwhile, Don Windsor ran out of the class, out of the playground and half way home before the teacher got over the shock. Sitting at the back of the class looking down the aisle, the whole incident looked like something out of a pantomime. He came in next day as if nothing had happened, greeting the teacher. They both went to Mr Coombs' study. Sometime later, they were back. Not a word was said, but Don had the making of a grin as he sat in his place. The teacher left two weeks later, a nervous wreck. On another later date we visited the

Camberwell School of Art. I can never recall how we came to be there. Was it crass stupidity by the school or did we go there after finishing woodwork tuition at the nearby Oliver Goldsmith School? Probably the former, who knows?

We entered the gothic pile into a vestibule, then on to a kind of gallery; works of art arrayed, sculptures, busts, statues, and, of course, pictures. Don Windsor was in his element. Someone tried to conduct us around, which didn't happen. Don went up to a nude life-sized Greek deity in stone, got behind her, cupped her breasts from behind, and went through the motions of goosing her, making guttural noises amid cheers from the rest of the lads. The attendant could do nothing until Don reached his climax and ceased, coming down from the pedestal. The poor man did his best to usher him on, but only after he had patted the rumps of every female statue. By the way, by this time we were in our last year.

Don was obviously enjoying himself and got ahead of the excited attendant to the part of the gallery containing pictures "ancient and modern". He exclaimed "Boys! Look at the tits on that!" We were then herded out by two attendants. Never again would anyone from our school be allowed into the Art School, by decree.

I partially blamed the authorities in the first place, for siting the Art School in Camberwell. Someone should have thought of founding the school in a more salubrious place, like Blackheath or Dulwich, leaving the good people of Camberwell and Peckham to their own prosaic ways. Thinking of our woodwork class nearby and Mr Oakin, our teacher, who told us of his life, coming from a long line of carpenters in Russia, driven out by the double eagled, military cavalry, practising their skills in England; full of stories of his Grandfather, who could look at a broken window glass and cut new glass without any measurement. We all liked him. If anyone made an error, he would shrug, and show whoever the right way with no fuss.

John Sparrow in our class was a big bloke but never bullied anyone. His mum was having another baby and needed a playpen, but couldn't afford to buy one. He explained to Mr Oakin that he would like to make one at school. Mr Oakin jiggled some figures when ordering the next batch of wood, and the class was told that we all had to ensure that in future there would be no off-cuts wasted, so we all learned the value of economy, and wasted nothing. Thus John made his forthcoming baby's playpen, and so ended up being expert at making mortise and tenon joints.

I met him in the late sixties, by chance in Sevenoaks. He was now a Master builder, very respected locally. We shook hands. I sang chu- chu- chu- chewing gum, reminding him of what our class sang whenever I turned up for school. He was embarrassed and went red; I laughed it off, then we sparred for a mock fight, saying we should keep in touch, but of course we never did.

I had made a few friends at school. One day, as I walked past some kids in the playground, some kid called out my name. I turned. "My name's Terry, I live in Sears Street". "Yes", I said, "Your dad has the car lot in New Church Road". We chatted and became mates, which lasted for the rest of the time whilst we were in school. His Dad was selling American jeeps – hardly used ex-war surplus for twenty-five pounds each. Farmers would travel into Camberwell to buy them, there being a shortage of tractors. He would buy any old cars and would get them driveable. There was no M.O.T. then, which made life easier.

My other mate was Eddy Rodmell. We were made milk monitors by nasty Mr Astill the art teacher,and now our form master. It meant collecting thirty-odd small bottles of milk and giving it out to the class, then collecting the empties back later. We hated doing it, but Mr Astill's word was law. If we complained about anything, he would sneer at us, telling us to get on with it or else. He also mimicked my stammer. He then made Eddy and me board monitors, cleaning and setting up his double size blackboard for the next art lesson, always moaning about anything he could find in front of the whole class. Some kids said to us "complain to the Headmaster", but they were mates from way back. We bided our time. I would knock for Eddy every morning on my way to school, waiting for him to wash himself wearing only a singlet, summer and winter. The only water tap was outside but Eddy was obsessed with being clean. He would find something clean to wear and we would finally get off to school early enough to do our setting up and cleaning the big blackboard. One day, having ridiculed me, Mr Astill turned on Eddy, calling him a dirty, scruffy urchin. This was too much for Eddy. Mr Astill had hit a nerve. With tears in his eyes he kept repeating over and over, do I look dirty, Dave? We came up with a plan.

Next day, setting up the cleaned blackboard, we inserted the wooden pegs into the holes, carefully placing the blackboard onto the pegs, then easing each peg outwards, the pegs just about holding the blackboard up. The class assembled. Mr Astill was not very tall and always had to reach to write from the top. By doing so, the blackboard flexed, the wooden pins flew out and the blackboard became a guillotine, coming down with such force onto his foot (we found out later) that he had two broken bones in his foot. The class were silent, watching him as he hobbled out of the classroom, red-faced, tears of pain in his eyes. No one helped. Silence. A while later the class reacted, cheering and shouting "Well done!". We denied everything, "it was an accident" we said. Some kids blew raspberries, comments were made.

They knew, for certain, but when an enquiry was held not one said it was anything but an accident.

He was away for two weeks, then toning down his attitude to the whole class: Good.

The odd ten minutes with Mr Benjamin here and there were working out well. He said my speaking was improving, which I hadn't noticed. I told him that I could not spell some of the alternative words that well. He had read a report from the Maudesley Hospital that I was partially dyslexic, among other things. He said this was not important, and said "spell words phonetically". I had read books at home – "The Cuckoo in the Nest" by Mrs Oliphant, and "Don Quixote" by Cervantes. Mr Benjamin taught us to analyse what we had read, the essence of what authors really meant in their writing. Clever.

Switching time again: one day my Aunt Doll was called to the school to do with her twins – my cousins. As she entered the school corridor, she was run over by Mr Green, our Games teacher. He knocked her to the ground. He had been warned about cycling too fast before in the corridors. After hasty apologies and a sweet cup of tea in the Headmaster's study, all was forgiven. Mr Green was a burly figure and had played rugby for Wales. Apart from his eccentric ways, he was well liked. His main agenda was cricket, football and P.T. Mr Coombs was reckoned to be scared of him. No wonder.

Behind our tenement block there was some waste ground. One day workmen turned up with bricks and mortar, and very quickly built an air-raid shelter, having an L-shaped wall at each end, hiding the doors from bomb blasts. It became a regular venue, filling up when the sirens went. One lady, a Mrs Baxter, had an enormous row with Mr Warner, who was responsible for the public shelter. She had, over time, moved her effects into the shelter, taking up too much room. She had brought her mattress and armchair, a tiny tripod paraffin heater, lamps, a candlestick, her canary in its cage, and then her cat, telling all that he was a good mouser. There was no gas or electricity within the shelter but somehow she managed to cook on the heater. Soon the place stank of Mrs Baxter's cooking, the cat, and of Mrs Baxter herself, who by now had taken up permanent residence. Some people said that it was better to stand outside in an air raid, facing the Luftwaffe than Mrs Baxter and her new home. The row went on for a few days. In the end, Mr Hardy got involved, and Mrs Baxter moved back, reluctantly. The smell persisted.

One night, the bombing was so loud, I rose from my little bed, and went upstairs to the flat roof where my Dad was fire watching. My Mum was on night shift still, she and her gang still making pontoon barges. I was caught on another night when both parents were working; my Dad had been called by Mr Hardy in an emergency. I awoke, dressed and walked towards Camberwell Green Market. There was rubble everywhere.

The Salvation Army was there in their tea cabin. I stood in the shadows. Everything was mayhem. I stood by where I had been used to stand; now just rubble. Someone spotted me. After giving my name and address, I was ordered to go home before the next air raid.

I never ventured out again.

One night the bombing woke me. I went up to where my Dad was fire watching. I stood on an upturned bucket so that I could look over the top of the parapet wall.

The sight was unearthly. Facing North towards the docks everything had turned orange. The whole of the Surrey Docks was on fire. It was one of the biggest timber wharves in England, and it played a large part in imported foodstuff, whatever. I looked up and could see the underside of the German bombers – they were flying so low that I could see the marks on the side of each plane, easy to see in the orange sky.

My Father by this time saw me: "You might as well stay on this roof" he said, always the fatalist. The fire lasted for days, acting like a beacon for the German bombers. The night sky was orange for quite a few nights; nothing could be done.

After the war, on special days, my Grandfather would "bull up" his uniform, etc. for the "Old Contemptibles" – old soldiers' reunion. He would burnish his boots, size 13 ½, heating up the black wax polish, then I watched whilst he applied the hot wax to his boots with the end of an old tablespoon.

I then had to walk him to the bus stop. By then he would have exercised his legs enough to be all right for the rest of the day. I would then tidy up their bedroom. Normally

my day started with going into our Gran next door, go up
and empty their commode, rinse and put back, tidy up,
dusting off the pictures of Queen Victoria, King Edward
and two King Georges. Sometimes I would massage my
Grandfather's lower back with "Goddards Horse Oil". It did
his back good, but it didn't do me any good. No matter how
many times I washed, I could still smell that embrocation
oil on me for the rest of the day.

The word would go around that Sun Pat had a delivery
of raw peanuts. As the hoist with a huge hook would take
the peanuts up three storeys they would then be pulled in
off the gantry. As the man on the track looked up, a kid
would pierce the next sack and dodge under the track. As
the sack was lifted, the hessian sack opened a bit more. Kids
appeared from nowhere. The idea was to grab some and
run for your life. You had to be a good runner if you lived
around our way.

Now the war was over. The kids in Lomond Grove
decided to have a victory celebration of their own. With
plenty of wood to start fires they soon amassed loads of
paper, wood – anything that would burn. All told, three
fires were started, each one in the middle of the road. A
few vehicles passed with much bad language. I went to the
corner and looked down at the fires. The kids seemed to
be having quite a good time, all three fires being stoked up,
there not being much traffic. Until "Chooka" Richardson
turned from New Church Road into Lomond Grove in his

Atkinson flatbed lorry. He was always in a hurry so he ran over all three fires as if they weren't there; the fires went everywhere. Chooka just kept going as if nothing had happened. He made things worse; his flatbed truck was petrol engine. I know that because whenever he couldn't pay his petrol account I used to take two cans to the petrol garage in Wyndham Road. The man serving the petrol would get suspicious of who the petrol was for. I had to think up a name. This is where my stammer could help, giving me time to make up a name and address.

The Richardsons lived in Caspian Street, so I gave a false name and address in Evelina Buildings. Another good thing about stuttering was that I could pull faces and make a few noises at aggressive people. Most would flinch and shy away, at a loss of what to do next. I thought this was ever so funny, and it got me out of trouble.

You have to make do with what you've got.

There lived opposite us in Westmacott Street a family called Butler-Smith and Owl. Jeanny Owl was over a year older than me. She had lived all over South east London. Mrs Butler, her Mum, dressed smartly, with always a lot to say. Mr Smith was a quiet man who seemed to be in the background. Mrs Butler-Smith and Owl was always telling my Mum and my Aunt Doll how much the Irish labourers all fancied her.

I would be ushered indoors, whilst she told stories which made my Mum and Aunt go agog.

The Irish gangs were well liked by everyone because they were always cheerful and worked hard at repairing bomb-blasted houses. During the war and after the war, many never went back to Ireland and settled down, got married, and later became builders.

One talented workman drew a sketch of Mrs Butler-Smith and Owl on a piece of board; it took on the persona of the Mona Lisa. The whole gang of them never went short of a cup of tea and a piece of toast – they earned it.

Later on in time, people started to dislike the Irish who came over to rebuild London and all of the big cities; housing was in crisis again. Many slept rough, causing ill feeling and hatred, soon to end when in a few years, West Indians started to arrive here, giving people someone new to hate.

Another story I feel strongly about.

Another day, yet another time, walking up the Denmark Hill towards the Odeon, nearly opposite the Camberwell Palace, there was this bookshop. I was intrigued.

I'd bought books for one penny each if worn, tuppence each for better books. The shop owner had bought a job lot after a shop had been blown up, but now I was ready for better things, or so I thought. I had a lot to learn. I stayed with the tuppeny books round the corner where we lived. I don't know why I mentioned this posh shop. Years later I became a regular customer. One day I picked up an Iliad – and started to read "This is the song of arms and the man",

I think. A voice behind me said "I think you should start with the Odyssey by Homer". He was right. I was hooked. The man that I thought was a "shirt-lifter" wasn't – lots of bookish people spoke like that. Nowadays no-one cares – most people are taken at face value, as it should be.

Not then.

Back at school, this year we were mainly in Mr Young's class. Apart from being a good teacher and a nice guy, he could not keep order in the class. Sometimes it was as if he was talking to himself. I still sat at the back of the class in the same position whatever classroom we were in. Burchmoor, was in his usual place at the back of the class. He had discovered masturbation. He would sit with his desk lid upright, thinking that he was invisible. He could not stop; when he finally did stop, tired, he would fall asleep. He was, in the class's opinion, passing his brain through the eye-hole of his own penis. One day I was called out to the front of the class. On the blackboard the teacher had drawn a stencil of the British Isles. "How many towns and cities can you identify?" I took the chalk, marked out Glasgow, Edinburgh, Manchester, Birmingham, all told about twelve principal towns and cities fairly accurately. When I gave back the chalk he said "Where did you learn all this?" pointing to the map. "Here Sir!" I shouted above the din. The poor man was confused. Also, he was on Mr Coombs' list.

One teacher, a Mr Watson, took us for a variety of subjects. Around his classroom were pictures of

Shakespeare, Marvel, Shelley and many others. Mr Watson would stop the class whilst he spoke to his pictures, with gaps left where they could answer back. The class would be silent whilst the pictures and Mr Watson had their conversation. The legend was that Mr Watson had been shell-shocked in the Great War, It was also said that he had been with Captain Scott on his attempted expedition to the South Pole, reaching as far as Camp five. No-one could say if there was any truth in this story. The school gave him the benefit of the legend, and so put up with his peculiar ways. One day, at break time, I was pinched hard on my backside. I shouted "Ouch!" I spun around to face Mr Watson, who said "there you are, Lillywhite, you did not stutter then, did you?" I often wondered if perhaps half the school, teachers and pupils should attend the Maudesley Hospital with me. At the end of each lesson period, he would hold his aged fountain pen in one hand and the pen cap in the other, trying and trying to connect his pen and its holder with shaking hands. It took minutes to connect. The class waited with bated breath; when he finally managed to complete the operation a sigh of relief came from the class. The lesson was now over and the class would rush out to the next lesson elsewhere.

He was not on the Headmaster's list for random caning.

Then on to Mr. Blayney's class for Mental Arithmetic. He kept his own cane and would cane anyone who got too many answers wrong. I was lucky as I was above average, so never got punished. D'Artagnan, alias Mr Coombs the Headmaster, never visited Mr Blayney's class.

No need.

Camberwell Palace was always known as a rough place – not just for the type of audience, but also for some of the performers. That's where my Grandfather came into his own. In his time, he was a front-of-house commissionaire to most of the West End theatres, where he was constantly opening doors to all kinds of people, keeping order, well-tipped by the patrons, and well-liked. He worked at times at the Camberwell Palace. His job description was "Official Quietener". Anyone playing up or causing trouble would hear the sound of his thirteen and a half sized boots coming down the aisle and would cease, but too late. The poor man would be whisked out of his seat and escorted from the Palace, his feet not touching the floor, to a round of applause, sometimes putting on a better show than the one on stage. My Dad was full of stories about him, when Granddad was younger.

Forward in time to the Maudesley Hospital. The kid who smoked passed the word that we should meet outside after the session. We walked clear of the hospital, stopping to say he'd heard that the doctors were going to make us take an intelligence test! Saying that if anyone failed, they could be "sectioned" and put into an asylum, if two doctors signed a form. We had, despite our different problems, formed an unlikely bond.

Yes, some time later we all had a one to one test. One question was "It has been reported in a newspaper that in a train crash, the end carriage always killed lots more passengers than the rest of the train. Therefore the railway companies will now take the end carriage off" – inviting a response. Of course, the answer would be – but there would always be an end carriage whatever – easy!

Another test was a square tray with four sides containing wooden bricks that fitted exactly with a gap with one cube missing in a corner of the tray. In the diagonally opposite corner was one red brick. The task was to move the red brick, which had to be moved over to the other diagonal corner in the minimum of moves. There were about twenty of this type of tests. Prior to this we all agreed to take our time and not to get flustered. Our group all came through and stayed together, bonding us even closer than before.

Once we were put into a large room full up with junk; old blackboards, wood, a square tank half filled with water, ropes and other impedimenta. We all filed in and were told that we could do whatever we liked. Some of the kids loved it, others weren't so sure. The kid that I sat with lit a roll-up. I scouted round the room. The outside wall had large windows, but I noticed that inside walls had none. I looked again. Easily missed because of the masses of rubbish. There were tiny horizontal windows at about four feet apart. There were no frames with the glass. There was no light on the other side – we were being watched from all sides, unnoticed. I ambled over to the kid I sat with and told him. He had been there longer than the rest of us. I suppose, in his way, he was the team leader.

He finished his roll-up, went to the others, told them what was going on and that we were being watched, and to tone down what they were doing. I often wondered if the doctors ever twigged. We started to go into Ruskin Park, and sat inside the old summer house folly, giving our own versions of what they were up to, having our own therapy!

I was ten years old, no eleven plus for me, but because I had read books one, two and three, it may have been decided to award me a prize for my efforts. I think that the only book left over was a detailed history of the War of the Roses. Other children received "Biggles" books – most popular were Famous Five and Billy Bunter, so I think I had a left over book. My Dad was very pleased, but for the life of me I could not get into that book. I eventually part exchanged by new book in the old shop in New Church Road for a couple of tuppenny ex-library books.

Exchange is no robbery.

One autumn day, being nice for a walk and towards the end of school holidays, I set off walking up to the Odeon. I branched right past Loughborough Junction to Electric Avenue, to the Brixton Town Hall, turning left and up by a skating rink. I stopped for a breather by a pub called the "George Canning". There in the forecourt was a beautiful car. I could only stare at it, I think that it could have been a Daimler, Rolls Royce, Bentley – a change from all old crocks that most people were driving. After some time, the man came from the pub, saw me and shouted "OYE, you bin touching that car???" I stammered "No sir, just looking. It's the best car I have ever seen, better than the King and Queen's" I related my seeing their car at Camberwell Green. "You think mine's better?" I nodded. We got talking about all sorts of things – he knew South London better than I did. I told him that I did totting in my spare time, finding all sorts of things. He laughed and said "It's nice to talk with you son" He put his hand into his pocket and gave me two shillings. "Get yourself some Tizer" He smiled, waved and drove off. I went home by tram. Some time later I was looking at my Dad's paper, the Daily Mirror. In it was an article on George Dawson, the scrap millionaire, the man that I had been talking to about totting with my barrow, and Peter my dog that I found. No wonder he laughed! And there he was, grinning at me from his picture. And he wasn't even posh.

The newspaper said it was known that he kept £20,000 under his bed for a bit of pocket money.

I bet the King and Queen didn't do that. I had never been in a bank, but I s'pose he had money in them all, Barclays, Westminster, Martin's, the lot!

I had once seen a lot of money when my Dad came back from the races in his prince of Wales check suit and his brown trilby hat. He threw a huge wad of white five pound notes up in the air and laughed as they floated down. These notes were called Flims, as they were printed on thin white paper. It was a race who could grab the most.

My Mum won.

My First Holiday

The next thing that I knew we went on holiday to Folkestone in Kent, a proper holiday, not like hop-picking holidays where everyone had to work. We stayed at a board and lodgings in a nice house under some huge brick railway arches. We soon got to know Folkestone quite well, the beach, the sands, the harbour and the Leas. I loved going up and down on the chair lift. My Dad said its proper name was a Funicular or something. Up on the Leas a brass band was playing whilst we sunbathed in deck chairs. My sister loved the sea, but I didn't like the taste of salt water. Yuck. My sister was no trouble and made little friends playing in the sea and making sand castles and always singing – driving me mad.

Whilst my parents dozed off I had to keep an eye on my sister playing in the sea. When they woke up, I'd go to the harbour and watch an old fisherman working in the very low arches close to the harbour wall. He would cook the whelks and other shellfish peeling the whelks from the shells. For an old man, he was very quick. He pulled one whelk out of its shell – it was orange in colour. He looked up and in his local Kentish burr told me "This is a broody whelk. If someone is ill, this will make 'em better".

I sometimes stayed with him for hours. At certain times

when the tide was fully out, we would climb down where the old fishing boats lay slightly over to one side. He told me that some boats had no engines now and weren't used. He would hammer wooden bungs he had made into the holes where the propeller had been, so they would float with the tide. All the boats were black-hulled and clinker built, and a mounted red sail at the rear. "Although the triangular sail was small, it helped with steering the craft", he said.

We used to have our main meal in a café called the Ensign. Two brothers and their wives ran the café. Between them there was a little boy. I never found out which were his parents – it didn't seem to matter. When we walked in he always made a bee line for me, showing me his toys – I had made a new friend.

It was busy in the Ensign, so his mums or dads had not much time for playing. So we took him out with us. Thus this cemented our friendship with his mums and dads. We would fetch him back tired out – even better for his family. I became Michael's brother whilst we were on holiday and he would never leave me alone. Towards the end of our twelve days holiday, Michael's family offered to put me up for a couple of weeks, food and lodging free, as I was good with Michael and he with me. It was settled. I had my own room with a single bed on the top floor of the café, perfect. So we went everywhere and anywhere, from ball games on the East Cliffe, watching the ferry train couple up a second locomotive to push the train back up the hill to London, or lying on the sand. My charge would never wander off. I think he was a bit lonely on his own. We got on well.

When finally at the station, going home, his two mums gave me a hug and some pocket money! Michael cried a bit as they waved me goodbye. I shall always remember the Ensign Café, and the nice family of five, lovely food. Back to my Mum's cooking! Still, it was nice to be home, even puddy our mad cat stretched his paws on my best short trousers and purred a bit. Back to school and smelly Pauline Gordon, phew!

The year is nineteen forty-seven. I know because it had been in the papers about Princess Elizabeth's engagement to the Duke of Edinburgh as he was now titled. This made me nearly ten years of age. I sat in my grandparents' house one evening after finishing my chores, taking their china hot-water bottles up to their bedroom, tidying up, having been to the Pub for their jug of porter ale which was now in a saucepan on the Kitchener oven warming up. It was time for my Granddad to read the Star newspaper to my Gran, a routine. When the reading was over, a discussion took place. "Kit" he said, "I don't know if this Duke of EDINBERG (as in iceberg) is good enough for her. He was a Greek prince before this, I hadn't heard of this before". My Gran said "Well, Bill, it's her choice. She will probably make something of him. After all, Bill, I had to make something of you!" This caused a heated few words. Granddad would read again out loud, whilst they drank their porter ale.

Mr Atlee and his government would be the next topic, and so it would go on until bedtime.

My Granddad read slowly, not being a good reader, and could just about write, but could add up all right.

I could now read better than he could – thanks to Mr Moxon at school. I would finish my half mug of porter, help my Gran up to bed, and go home next door, through the back gate. I used to moan sometimes about doing for them every night, errands; putting Granddad's bits on whatever, but then would think of all the times they looked after me during the war when my mum and dad were doing their bit for the war effort.

In later years I read Milton's *"They also serve who only stand and wait"*.

During the war, I suppose this line of poetry applied to all of us, even me. I mean to say, collecting shrapnel, stacking cleaned up bricks for re-use is what most kids did, well they did round our street anyway.

A few old men cleaned the bricks where the fish and chip shop used to be, while we stacked. Good fun.

After the war was over and I had grown a bit, I would go with my Dad, meeting him at Aldgate. We would walk to Billingsgate fish market. The bummarees could carry boxes of fish on top of their funny hats, some pushing barrows up Fish Street Hill, with some down and outs helping to push the heavy carts up the hill. Everyone was busy. An order of nuns had first claim on any fish that had fallen on to the cobble stones, thus feeding the poor. When they left, my Dad would let me scoop up any mangled fish they didn't want. My Dad would wear his Corporation peaked cap with the City of London badge. He knew most of the people who worked there, so it was OK for me to shovel up squashed up fish into my big carrier bag with my little seaside shovel I had found. I reckon I was doing my bit to help the City of London, keeping the market clear. Sometimes we would have a cuppa in one of the funny little cafes, tucked away where you would never find them. One café had food called brotche or something. It was like an almost blue-black soup on what looked like mashed potatoes. No-one minded my big bag of mushy fish as everyone smelled of fish anyway. After our tea we would walk back to Aldgate where I would catch the forty-two bus home, leaving my Dad.

He always had other little jobs to do, or people to see, and would get home later. Passengers on the bus would not sit too close to me, and pulled faces. I didn't mind. At home, my mum would order me into our garden. I had found a "hopping pot" on my trails. It was made of iron with two handles and had an oval lid. Hop pickers used these for cooking and washing clothes and boiling their water, in fact everything, whilst picking in the hop gardens of Kent.

I would bone all the fish, then light a fire from my stock of wood and cook a big pot-load. This would last the dog and cat for quite some time. You should see their noses twitch – they loved it! My mum would make sure I was first in our old tin bath when I had finished cooking. I could not see the point of it all, I was always grubby doing other things. Ah Well.

Returning to the Country Holiday Fund, I was sent to Norfolk, to a place called Little Acre, near Castle Acre. There were two of us – a fair-haired kid who came from Naylor Road Peckham. His name was Vince. The old couple we stayed with were nice enough, feeding us, leaving us to our own devices. For breakfast we were given bread and milk in a bowl. We both hated it, but ate it up, knowing that was all there was. Then out to explore the castle and a huge abbey that also had been pillaged and deserted over the years. We made friends with local kids who took us to different places every day.

It was good not to see any bomb debris anywhere. Vince and I shared a bedroom which was OK. One morning the old man came into our room holding a cut-throat razor. We were both shocked and scared, where we came from this could only mean one thing.It turned out that his razor was his prize possession, made in Sheffield and was as good now as it was forty years before.

We hastily admired it. This was the old man's way of breaking the ice. We soon became part of the household and would sometimes go to Castle Acre township with them, and to Swaffham by charabanc!

We would pass Italian prisoners of war, who were kept on to work on the farms. They were hard workers and were well liked. Of an evening, before curfew, they would clean up and go to the local pub, wearing their blue/green uniforms (I am slightly colour blind between these two colours). The overcoats were like a cape over their shoulders, which gave them a continental look. The only thing that spoiled the effect was a big circle on the back of the coat, a kind of orange-yellow, denoting they were P.O.W.s;

They would sing in Italian as they walked, charming the local girls who were sometimes seen up one of the Castle ramparts with them. I bet a lot of the P.O.W.s never went home.

Some days I would go with the old lady into Castle Acre to the shops for groceries. One day, I was in a queue at a counter when a farmer came in, dressed in a tweed suit, pork-pie hat, wearing leather gaiters. He walked up to the queue, looked hard at a lady in front of me in her late forties, dressed up in a nice blouse and skirt. He walked in front of her, stopped and with both hands fondled her ample bosoms. She was a buxom woman. "You've a nice pair of titties there" he said. She was outraged – well almost. Did he know her? She did, calling him by name, perhaps it was some form of greeting in these parts, or had he been milking his cows and got carried away with what he had done. When she had called him a few names, he got onto the back of line. No-one batted an eyelid. I put the whole thing down to a Norfolk tradition.

In my dotage I went back to the area. Now the National

Trust or English Heritage have fenced everything off, the big monastery and the castle, adding a tea room and gift shop; where do the children play? Progress should be ashamed

The local people were kind to us, and I was sad when we left.

The next place I went to was in Hampshire, on a small farm. The lady's son was at boarding school, her husband was an officer in the Royal Navy at Portsmouth, only coming home at weekends. Good, because he smacked me hard for talking to the Gypsies. You could hear them coming up the lane, for as the caravan came toward us, all their pots and pans hooked on the underside made a Clunkaty Clunk, as they went to their campsite where by an old law they could only stay for twenty-four hours. When I had finished the jobs that the lady of the house got us to do, I walked along to the end of the lane where there were lots of trees bordering a large round field. It always looked clean and tidy, ready for the next lot of Gypsies.

Sometimes the same ones came back after a day or two. I'd go to the farm gate and wave, following them up and help them unpack. First thing was to feed and tend to their horse, next the head man would cut a large patch of turf, roll it up and store it. Next we would scout round the trees looking for wood and twigs and start a fire over a bare patch of earth, cut from under their caravans or vargers or something as they called them. Soon they would start to cook; the fire was shaped like a wigwam not giving much smoke. Everything they did had a reason. I learned many things from the gypsies. They spoke a language called Romany, only using a form of English when they spoke to me. It sometimes took a while to understand. No-one minded my stammer, the kids said that I was "cushty cosh" which I think meant that I was OK. They used lots of water. Our farm would give them none, some did further down the lane. I knocked on doors with my new mates and was given access to a well. We'd fill up the old milk churns, load onto our hand trolley and then back to the encampment.

Watching them all making clothes pegs was a wonder. The only tools needed were an axe, a sharp knife, a hammer and some scissors. Even small kids helped.

When they moved on, you would not think that anyone had ever been there. They would say, about any rubbish, "Beat 'em, burn 'em, bury 'em". The last thing would be re-laying the turf.

Then they were off. Sometimes there were three or four at a time, they would all come at the same time.

I loved it. The couple at our farm didn't. These Gypsies had hold of a Gorgio kid, who helped – that was Me! Even the kids could snare rabbits for the pot. They never went hungry.

When the Commander was on leave from the Royal Navy, his wife told him of me being friendly with the Gypsies up the lane. He got angry. In defence, I answered back saying I hadn't done any wrong. He was angry even more, and slapped me hard round the face, calling me a common little sod. I left the room in tears, only to speak to them again when something required an answer. I think his wife was glad to see the back of me. The only thing I missed when I left there were the Gypsies and a badger I saw in a shady forest one day. I stood stock-still watching its antics, marvelling at its black and white coat. He must have woken up early, making my afternoon.

Before I left, I met the son of the family. He was timid and quiet; had his father made him like it? Maybe that is the way posh people carry on. I was very glad to be back in Westmacott Street.

Another trip down memory lane: when we had settled down back at our old school after the war, the school doctor would appear with Nitty Nora, Jungle Explorer, as she was known, an old nurse who combed our hair with her flea raker. We hated the fine teeth cutting into our scalps. The doctor would do his bit. Without getting out of his chair, he would grasp our elbows, lifting us up about 6 inches off the floor – his way of weighing us. He would then bark at the nurse, now his secretary, "Malt, milk, or cod liver oil". Some kids got all three; the cod liver oil was awful, but later it was mixed with orange juice.

I was always in front of Pauline Gordon, for whom the nurse would take her off for a medicated shampoo with some other kids. I foolishly told my Mum about the whole session. She sprang into action, scrubbing my hair so much, making the flannel feel like emery paper. Having the working class preoccupation with dirt didn't help much. Then at school we would have exercise, dancing in the main hall. Each boy had to have a girl to dance with. I always seemed to have Pauline Gordon, as we skipped to the sound of a polka called "Sven the Cobbler". I have never liked that tune since.

The bad winter of 1947 was awful. It snowed heavily and shortly after we had a thaw. The streets were mushy, but before the thaw could do its work, every street turned to ice, the worst in living memory, turning the slushy streets into a death trap. St Giles Hospital was full of people with severe broken limbs and pneumonia. Death was common. No graves could be dug; it kept snowing so bodies were stored in the extreme cold, "preserving them", my Dad said. There was no food, no coal, our gas lamps hardly worked. When our coal ran out, we dug out coal dust from our coal hole under the stairs, me doing the inaccessible places at the back. My Dad mixed up the coal dust with water and cement and shaped them like dumplings. When dried, they burned quite well. I retrieved my barrow, got the wheels to turn, then toured the empty bombed houses where I knew there would be dry timber. We never went short of kindling or firewood. I'd have to hang on to the shafts of my barrow to stop myself slipping on the uneven ice. My Gran and Granddad stayed in bed for days, unable to keep any body heat.

One day our local milkman came to our street with a huge shire horse pulling a long pole ladder on which milk crates were picked up all the way along the ladder. It was a wondrous sight, the shire horse had a kind of overcoat on and some special spiked boots on his hooves.

How the milkman turned into Caspian Street was a marvel. Because we paid our milk bills on time, we were allowed extra milk, as it would keep for ages in the ice. It was weeks before things got better.

The undertakers were kept busy at last.

Fortunately Puddy and Peter were not fussy what they ate, nothing was wasted in our house. My mother would buy the cheapest meat – breast of lamb, mostly soft bone and lots of fat, smuggled out to our dog and cat when my Mum turned her back. We had an old copper boiler in our scullery. I would fetch in blocks of iced snow from the garden and melt it in our copper boiler. Our water pipes had frozen over for almost a month, but by then lots of water mains had burst. Even the King and Queen had to make cuts. Everyone moaned about the Government, but then got on with it. Mr Cripps in the Labour government said on the wireless that we all had to "tighten our belts".

We already had. Sometimes on walking up Westmacott Street just before Ernie the Barbers, there was a wide alley leading down to a tee junction either side of the vinegar factory were more houses and even more in the sides of the tee junction, each side going to a cul de sac. Most of

the tiny front garden fences had been burnt in the harsh
winter. I was doing an errand for Mrs Taylor, who looked
after me during the war when I was little, so I would call in
from times to time. Her friend was poorly, so I would take
food to her, plus anything else. She lived in the left branch
of the alley. In the middle of the "Tee" junction there lived
a woman and her young son. Summer and winter he would
wear a girl's tartan pleated skirt and a little white singlet. As
he ran about, throwing an old tin plate up in the air, he was
the light of her eye. She always greeted me with a smile and
spoke to me like I was an adult. She was tall, big boned, and
I think a bit lonely. Most people in the cul de sac ignored
her. "I have to find him tartan skirts and singlets, like the
man on the back of the porridge box, who wears a kilt, as
he throws a discus in the Highland Games. He wants to be
like him, it's the only way I could make him eat his breakfast
oats!" We laughed. He was always out with his mum who, I
found out, worked nearby in the vinegar factory. I wonder
what happened to them? Funny how your mind wanders.
Her neighbours would have been richer if they had passed
the time of day with this woman and her son.

I'm glad I did.

Later on, our King died; everyone was choked. At school,
in assembly, Mr Coombs gave a speech to a silent hall and
ended by saying that all pupils and staff will wear something
black during the time of mourning. The next day, kids came
in with bits of black ribbon tied to their sleeves, around

their collars like a tie, anything they could find. No-one laughed. George the Sixth was dead, but a school full of Georges lived on.

Amen.

Just after the end of the war, a film crew arrived looking round our area to find a place to show their models off to the best advantage, finally picking on a bomb-site near Notley Street, two turnings from us. The head man started to order people about, which didn't work. Local people were quite sullen. On came the models in fur coats, pill-box hats with a backdrop of debris and carnage. Now the film crew, were acting superior, at the same time patronising, and blocking the street.

The locals had enough. One woman told them all to bugger off, others joined in, using stronger language. The photographing stopped.

A man stepped forward, telling the crew that a lot of people had died round here, and you lot have no respect. They left quickly.

My Canadian aunt sent me a Zoot Suit. These were worn by black people in Harlem, and the style took off. Not so in England. My Mum and Dad made me wear it. The suit, a long drape jacket, trousers baggy below the waist, tapering at the knee then down to wide turnups or cuffs. My Aunt had also thrown in a lurid painted tie. I will be kind and say that the suit was two sizes too big. I wore the suit twice and made it plain to my Mum and Dad – "no more".

They relented, buying me my first long trousers, ready for changing schools.

I started a routine on Sundays. Now that I was nearly grown up in my trousers, I would walk one bus stop by Saint Gemma's Ladies' Dosshouse, that walk of one bus stop saved me money on the fare stage. I'd catch a number twelve bus to Westminster Bridge, saving more money by getting off on the south side of the Thames. More people should do this, their health is better when walking.

I would vary the routes, walking around Parliament Square, then down Whitehall, Trafalgar Square, then onto Northumberland Avenue back to the Embankment, looking over to the blitzed South Bank. It looked forlorn; the only thing standing was the old shot tower. It resembled a lighthouse with no light on top, instead, in bygone days, molten lead was poured down inside, raining down musket balls. So much to see, if you know where to look. Coal colliers, their trip nearly over from the Tyne and Wear, feeding the great Battersea Power Station with its coal. Those little ships, dipping their funnels under the bridges, almost in silent homage – the real meaning of "Coals from Newcastle" – who knows?

I was looking over the Thames one day between Waterloo Bridge and Westminster, when suddenly a huge shape came to the surface. I stood shocked into just staring in wonderment – the monster was moving fast, up the Thames, so it had to swim through to the most polluted river in England. All sides of the Thames were dumping grounds for sewerage and chemical effluents. In places the stench was overpowering. This monster had lived through it. I wished it well. Once past Chiswick, the water would be clear. I looked about me – there was no-one to talk to – it was too early for sightseers. I normally did not talk to anyone, and no-one spoke to me. That's how I preferred it to be.

I walked up to Hungerford Bridge, crossed over and walked up Villiers Street and back to Trafalgar Square, remembering at the end of the war there were two fighter planes, one in each fountain on chocks. The crowds threw money into the water and every penny went to the R.A.F. Benevolent Association.

An older man in waders scooped the money up with a kind of perforated spade. He was kept busy.

My Dad said the country was broke but people still gave to good causes. There were no M.P.s in government cooking the books as there was no money in the kitty to fiddle with.

During the Blitz many people who could afford to leave would lock their houses up and move into a house in the country far away from any war zone.

Finally, when peace was declared, they moved back to find their London house was now occupied by two families sharing. The authorities turned a blind eye. During the war, the Gear family lived three houses past us. They were a nice family who pitched in to help when needed. Then one day they just weren't there any more. When I asked about them, I was hushed up.

Later, it turned out that their surname was Ghia. Mr Ghia's real name was not Henry but Heindrich. His wife's name was not Hilda but Heidi. I never saw them again. When told to keep quiet over something, everyone did.

This is a kid's eye view of how people coped during and after World War Two in towns and cities.

Our country cousins in the same situation as us "townies" coped, but in a slightly different way; poaching, knowing what could be eaten from hedgerows, larger gardens now turned over to allotments, keeping quiet about the occasional pig in the back of the garden, or even a sheep. Rabbits to a good countryman could be caught expertly, along with mushrooming and using many other items in the food chain. Thus our country cousins coped.

Town dwellers could not do this or had any expertise to survive, so we in the large towns had to adapt as best we could, often sailing against the wind, lawfully or otherwise. No-one was unscathed from these practices, up and down through any class system.

Throwing food away was now a criminal offence; if caught the offender could be heavily fined. I think that no-one ever was. Who knows?

Harris Cakes after the war, was renamed Mr Kipling, and had been known to sell off broken hardtack biscuits, not only feeding the British forces and allies, but also lots of folk in south east London with the leftovers unfit for the services. All that was needed was a penny Oxo, making the beginning of a stew, adding whatever.

The Marble Arch Motor Cycle Stores was in Camberwell Green by the post office. Older boys would buy a worn out old crock for a few pounds, put a Guinness label in the tax disc holder, insure the bike for a couple of pounds, then ride off as easy as that. No checks – nothing.

When finally the old bike's engine started giving up, it would be driven over Wells Way canal bridge down onto the towpath, whilst still moving would jump off, run with the accelerator revved up, steering the machine into the middle of the canal. Another Viking funeral. All this was witnessed by other bike riders, who would take him to the police station where it would be declared stolen – all done in the best possible taste. Then on to the insurance office to claim his pay-out, then back to the Marble Arch to start the process all over again.

In the nineteen sixties the Surrey Canal was drained. Sitting on an old chair was a B.B.C. reporter called Fife Robertson surveying the whole canal as far as the eye could see. There they were, "stolen" motor bikes, ditto push-bikes, safes of all shapes and sizes, some with holes in them, others with their doors blown open, cash tills by the dozen, prams and pushchairs, each with a story to tell.

I will say no more.

There was another motor cycle shop in Stockwell trading

in a similar way but bigger, called "Pride and Clarkes", soon to be renamed, transmogrified by the local populace into "Snide and Sharks".

Another renamed café in Peckham Rye Lane rejoiced in the name of "Rumbling Tum". But not for long, seemingly doing better, only after the café started to be called –

"The Tumbling Bum".

God bless working class humour, Amen.

Backpedalling to the years back at school, in our third year no-one in class seemed to mind me being there or not. It was accepted. In front of the school there stood a lone building out of bounds, used by a Peckham girls school for cookery and domestic sciences. The girls marched in a "crocodile" into the playground only when the boys had gone in for assembly. It could only be Donald Windsor who brought in a shoe-box full of stag beetles which he managed to empty round the girls' rooms causing havoc. What we didn't know was that Don fancied one of the Peckham schoolgirls.

Whilst the stag beetle mania was on, the upset girls were told to wait in the playground shed. It was here that Don offered his services to their teacher. He was in, and soon rounded up the offending monsters, encouraged by his new girl friend.

God loves a trier.

The Morphing of Terry Tuck

I kept friends with Terry Tuck all through school. He was witty, funny, and a good mimic. Not seeing him for some time, I paid him a visit. A young woman opened the door wearing a red dress, matching high heels, crowned by long dark hair. Yes, it was Terry. The whole family made me welcome, glad that I didn't seem to mind. "We don't let him out like it his mum said. It must have been awful for people like Terry in the early fifties – most people's attitudes were hostile, to say the least.

Brian Boyle, whom I liked, came from a big Irish family. His younger brother was "queer" so when I asked of him, Brian said "Oh no, he isn't queer any more". Dad gave him a good hiding. Beating up people seemed to be the answer to most things. If only it was that easy.

Our last term at school went quickly, having a dialogue with our teachers on lots of subjects. Donald Windsor had found out that Mr Young and his girlfriend played tennis on the hard court at Ruskin Park every Wednesday evening. One session involved an audience of half our class, applauding wildly at every move that Mr Young or his lady friend made. Don was always the cheer leader.

I often wondered if Mr Young profited from our educating him or vice versa. Anyway, Mr Young had survived us which was remarkable.

When school broke up for the last time, the leavers queued outside of Mr Coombs' office to receive our last report, given to us by the school secretary. Shocked when opened, for inside the envelope was a fantastic report concerning my endeavours, achievements, general conduct, all of which did not exist. We had all opened our reports and all stood in the corridor in a state of shock; our reports were a work of fiction. Whose handwriting was it? Had he paid someone to write everyone's report?

Mr Coombs was nowhere to be seen, probably on his rounds, caning a kid or two, just to keep in practice for a new intake. Even Donald Windsor got a good report; as he read it he was heard to shout "Lies, lies".

I had never seen him so angry.

After the war it was time to get back to normal, so we had pie and mash in Arnotts in the Walworth Road; it was always busy. I would sometimes go there on my own. It was quite famous in our part of London, but you had to queue. In the kitchen area you could see the pies being cooked, half by steaming and then oven-baked, with a huge vat of liquor simmering by the side of a machine for mashing potatoes. Pure mass production. After shouting my order, which would be two ice cream scoops of mashed potato, a steaming hot pie, followed by a scoop of liquor made of Arnotts' own recipe (a mixture of milk, water, chopped parsley and flour) one ladle per person. When paying you were then given a spoon. It was an unwritten law, having waited for a seat, the punters would eat quickly, leaving their seat for someone else. Anyone who lingered too long would be told politely that their seat was needed. Other diners on the same bench seat stood up when vacant, letting the new diner sit against the wall whilst finishing their pie and mash, making their seat free as soon as possible. No one stood for long. When finished everyone would take their plate to the counter with their spoon to be checked by the lady working the dishwasher, in case people thought they could take them home – no chance. The only other dishes were jellied eels. They were nice but a lot dearer. The sawdust on the floor was changed regularly. I would leave my barrow outside where I could keep an eye on it. I suppose, in a way, pie and mash shops were a forerunner of today's MacDonald's.

Feeding the Masses.

The ancient Greeks, in their infinite wisdom, may have invented PI, but it was the British that invented Pie. Yes, the British I am proud to say.

I read once that anyone below the rank of Baron was banned by law from eating pies, with the exception of "humble pies" made with the intestines, hearts and other unmentionable parts. Whilst the "upper crust" ate and dined well on the prime meat in their pies, even five and twenty blackbirds, anyone caught eating pies above their station were put into the stocks or fined.

Well, back to the forties. On each of the marble topped tables would be placed a Tizer bottle, a hole drilled through the stopper. Hot pepper seeds and vinegar in each one, next to the vinegar bottle there would be a huge salt cellar in the shape of an old tankard, its domed lid perforated.

Some people asked for a knife and fork; they got them, but were treated with suspicion. Cutlery was not easy to find in the early post-war years. As you have probably realised, I was always hungry, as most kids were, so in all the time that I would eat in the pie shop, I never heard one complaint from anyone waiting for a seat, nor from any other quarter. So be it.

I was about eight years old when my Dad gave me a rabbit, payment for his services to someone local. It was very young, so I kept it in a straw box out in our scullery. He became very friendly, even towards Peter and Puddy. I soon found some timber and mesh and made a nice large hutch with a small bedroom and a large play area. I named him Blacky on account of he was blue-black all over. Feeding was no problem as I was good mates with the mongol bloke who sorted all the vegetables out on his Dad's stall. I could fill my barrow with bits of swede, apple, potato, bits all boiled up in my hopping pot. I added bran to the pot making, when boiled down, a mash. My Gran next door saved potato peel for me. Everything went in the pot. Blacky, Puddy and Peter ate it and our chickens ate some too.

Coming home from school, the first thing was to let Blacky out to run round the garden. All the animals didn't seem to mind him; Blacky, on the other hand, would run and do flying somersaults with excitement then spend time looking at the chickens through the mesh. Sometimes I had to chase him round our garden when it was his bed-time. It became a game, one of many.

One lunchtime I rushed in from school. My meal was ready so I tucked into it; for a change it was well cooked. The meat was fine, until I noticed it was baked rabbit! I vaulted out into the garden. Blacky's hutch was empty. I stood there numbed, working out that my Mum had got home that day from her office cleaning job, took Blacky through the gate to my Granddad's shed and he, unbeknown, had killed my pet rabbit, skinned and gutted it. Poor old Blacky. She would have paid Granddad his sixpence. End of story, but not for me. I went indoors, not listening to my Mum's mean excuses, tipped my plate onto the floor, swore at my Mum, and ran back to school, two corners and three streets away, not caring about the trouble I was going to be in, over what I had called my Mum. When I finally went home, nothing was said, so I said nothing.

My Dad couldn't look me in the eye.

I grew up a lot that day.

Shortly after this my industrious Mum decided to paint our outside lavatory with a pot of green paint, probably left over from her war job painting pontoon barges. The paint was awful, possibly sub-standard. She painted the wall to wall, seat, the pipes, the cistern, finally the door-handles and catches. Now no-one could use the lavatory. To make things worse the U.S. paint would not dry for days, which meant that we had to use my Gran and Granddad's loo, thereby causing a few rows, to say the least.

It was shortly after this episode that the cat ran off with the bacon ration, causing my mother to shake her fists at our cat Puddy, as he calmly ate the bacon, out of reach. Not to inflame the situation, I kept mute, but inside was shaking with laughter.

He who dares wins, Puddy.

Technology finally came to Westmacott Street in the shape of a machine for sharpening knives, axes, drill bits and anything needed for cutting.

The cutler had put a lot of thought into his sharpening machine. He would sit on the handles, placing a length of wood across to make a seat. He would work the treadle underneath the barrow, like a large sewing machine.

He told the kids watching "Any kid who brings me something to be sharpened will get a lollipop". He prospered his sharpening wheels never stopped in Westmacott Street.

Going back a bit. One day I met a kid in the same line as me – totting. He lived in Walworth and covered the "Elephant" area. His barrow had four wheels and a chassis from a pram with springs under it, with a fruit box from Covent Garden. I said that his barrow was nice, he said the same about mine. I think we both lied. My barrow had two bigger and stronger wheels and was very good for a quick getaway. His barrow was too cumbersome and would not steer very well. Anyway, we got on well enough to tell me his "uncle" bought ties for tuppence and threepence each, according to condition. His uncle lived in a closed up shop near the Albany Road. His wife washed the ties, re-pressed them, they then had cellophane slips made to fit the ties into – the slip had "Reno Ties" diagonally down the front of each pack – they were now ready for East Street Market.

I always got paid well for the ties that he bought which he sold at two and sixpence each, up to three shillings. Some people brought them back complaining that the ties were worn behind the collar, saying they weren't new. The kid's "uncle" would tell the punter that the word "Reno" was not a posh place in America, but that Reno was short for renovated.

End of story.

But when Reno ties came to an end, "Uncle" had found a new line; this was obsolete paper roses, red, yellow, pink and blue in a papier mache tray of four. They were hideous, no-one wanted them, but "Uncle" bought them all for pennies, his shop stacked to the ceiling with them. When I visited him one day, he was spraying the paper roses from a FLIT gun made of tin. He poured into the FLIT reservoir a mixture of D.D.T., pine disinfectant and some smelly essence, probably got from Baldwin's at the Elephant and

Castle, giving the whole cocktail a pleasant enough effect. He was going to sell them around the markets as fly-killing air fresheners. As each one was sprayed then put into cellophane slips. I cannot remember the writing printed on the slips. Once the slips were on they were ready for market, where they flew off his stall at two shillings a tray, turning the woebegone paper roses into a very profitable Dunkirk.

Carpe Diem.

My earliest recollection was when being about three years old I was with my parents visiting an uncle and aunt at Golford with their family, who were hop-picking, and had been for a few generations on Middleton and Lovett's Farm opposite. As I tottered along the unmade cart-track I slipped and fell head first into a deep muddy rut, caused by the horsedrawn hop wagons. I called to be picked up. No-one took any notice. I glanced upward, to see my Mum and Dad and the rest of our family standing, looking skyward, oblivious to my shouts. Years later, walking the same route I realized why they ignored me all those years before. The whole family had been watching a part of "the Battle of Britain".

I am at the end of this narrative of an earlier life. Just an outline of what kids like me living in other Westmacott Streets in towns and cities all over England got up to, and survived.

I have no philosophy to impart, no author's message. Over my long years I have chanced upon Messrs. *Socrates,*

Bertrand Russell, Nietzsche, and many others of their ilk, and confess to have not one Iota of what they are on about.

I have to say that it seems to me there is a need for philosophy as a vehicle between groups of intelligent people to guide the rest of us, of average intelligence through life, including myself as being hopefully normal.

So Be It.

David Lillywhite

Lightning Source UK Ltd.
Milton Keynes UK
UKHW011140040522
402370UK00002B/71